MIX
PRO
AUDIO
SERIES

SOUND FOR PICTURE

An Inside Look at Audio Production For Film and Television

Editors: Jeff Forlenza and Terri Stone
Series Editor: David Schwartz

Hal Leonard Publishing Corporation

Library of Congress Catalog Card Number: 92-074789

These articles were previously published in a somewhat different form in *Mix* magazine.

Book design by Michael Zipkin.

Production staff: Brad Smith, general manager; Todd Souvignier, editorial manager; Georgia George, production director.

Thanks to *Mix* editors: Adam Beyda, Blair Jackson, Tom Kenny, Carolyn McMaster, George Petersen, Paul Potyen.

Cover photos (clockwise from left): Actor Tim Robbins in *The Player*, ©1992 New Line Productions Inc. All rights reserved. Photo by Lori Sebastian. Photo appears courtesy of New Line Cinema Corp. On location from *The Abyss*, ©1989 Twentieth Century Fox Film Corp. All rights reserved. Skywalker Ranch Foley stage, courtesy of Lucasfilm Ltd. Mix One Room, EFX Systems, Burbank, CA; photo by Ruben Araiza.

MIXBOOKS
6400 Hollis St., Suite 12
Emeryville, CA 94608
(510) 653-3307

MixBooks is a division of Act III Publishing

Printed in Winona, Minnesota, USA

ISBN 0-7935-2002-9

Table of Contents

v   **Introduction**
by Tom Kenny

vii   **Foreword**
by Francis Ford Coppola

FILM Theory

2   **The Art of Soundtrack Design**
by John Michael Weaver

7   **Sound for the Visual Medium**
by Randy Thom

12   **Post-Production Pioneer James G. Stewart**
by John Michael Weaver

18   **Creating Sound Effects**
by Blair Jackson

24   **Sound Designers and Digital Post**
by Blair Jackson

FILM Applications

30   **Terminator 2**
by Tom Kenny

36   **Malcolm X**
by Tom Kenny

42   **Beauty and the Beast**
by Tom Kenny

48   **The Hunt for Red October**
by Frank Serafine

54   **The Player**
by Tom Kenny

57   **Indiana Jones and the Last Crusade**
by Nicholas Pasquariello

62   **The Abyss**
by Iain Blair

66   **The Doors**
by Tom Kenny

TELEVISION Theory

74   **Mixing for Live Broadcast**
        by Bob Clearmountain

82   **Video for Audio Formats**
        by Tom Kenny

89   **Time Code Basics**
        by Eric Wenocur**

TELEVISION Applications

94   **The Simpsons**
        by Dan Daley

98   **Northern Exposure**
        by Richard Maddox

103   **The Wonder Years**
        by Amy Ziffer

108   **Twin Peaks**
        by Blair Jackson

111   **The Arsenio Hall Show**
        by Brad Leigh Benjamin

116   **Academy Awards**
        by Amy Ziffer

APPENDICES

124   **CD Production Music and Sound Effects Libraries**
        by George Petersen

128   **Glossary**

131   **Photo Credits**

133   **Acknowledgments**

Introduction

"SEE A DOG, HEAR A DOG." For years, this was the informal Hollywood maxim governing the relationship of sound to picture. Sound editors, mixers, supervisors—they all muttered the phrase in an effort to reveal the very real limits on their creativity and the very real demands of the storytelling process. You still hear the phrase today as you walk into a dub stage or through an audio post-production house, though it is now usually prefaced by, "It used to be…"

Picture is primary, no question. We are a visually oriented society, and we are forced to look at images in a way that we are not forced to hear sounds. As John Michael Weaver suggests in "The Art of Soundtrack Design," try walking down a city street with your eyes closed (and with a friend), absorbing the intricate and complex urban rush of sounds. Suddenly your ears open up. Maybe a tire squeal leaps out, or the idling diesel engine of a truck unloading its daily supplies makes you pause for just a moment, or the smell of fresh bagels implies clanging oven doors. All sorts of new possibilities emerge for matching sound to picture, some of them obvious, some not.

Every sound recordist, editor or mixer who understands the craft also understands that the soundtrack is but one element of a production. The sharpest, most subtle, most creative sound elements mean nothing if they detract from the overall goal, which is the telling of a story. In one of the more ironic statements coming out of the audio community, many of the top sound designers working today have said, "I know I've done my job if I'm not heard, if I'm not noticed."

Sound cannot be distracting if it is to be an equal partner to picture, but that does not mean that sound cannot be applied creatively. Today, you may see a dog and hear a dog—augmented by lion growls or trumpet blasts. You may see a dog and hear only crickets. Or, in one of the more dramatic scenes in recent cinema, you may see Al Pacino walk into a restaurant to kill a rival in *The Godfather*, while hearing only the piercing screech of the elevated train as it rounds a bend.

Sound has always been used creatively by those who work with picture. What a shock it must have been to hear *The Jazz Singer* in 1927. And what a thrill it must have been to be working in the film studio sound departments in those early days of the talkies. James G. Stewart, profiled here and whose career in film and television sound spanned six decades, was certainly every bit as creative as those who turned out the stellar sound design for *Terminator 2* or *Beauty and the Beast* or *Twin Peaks*. The technology was more limiting in the 1930s, but the imagination that made use of that technology was not.

Today, thanks to technology, editors work with more precision and speed. The current crop of digital audio workstations, sound effects libraries and digital video formats has created a mini-boom in the audio post-production industry as directors and producers shop around for the services that fit their particular needs. But the technology is only a tool, as you will read in the following pages, and there is always a new box just around the corner. Creative *people* drive the industry.

In this collection of articles on sound for picture, we present the sound artist and audio technology, with insights on how they interact to bring a story to the screen. What works on Saturday morning animation does not necessarily work in prime time. What works for Robert Altman doesn't necessarily work for Oliver Stone. What works in New York doesn't necessarily work in Los Angeles. There are no *correct* ways of working in sound for picture. Sometimes you may see a dog and hear nothing. Sometimes silence can be the most powerful sound of all. — *Tom Kenny*

Associate Editor

Mix magazine

Foreword

WHEN I WAS A CHILD of five, I was taken into the soundproof glass booth of studio 8H at the RCA building to watch my father play flute in the Arturo Toscanini NBC Symphony Orchestra. My focus went immediately to a large, black wheel, which, when turned in one direction, filled the room with the sound of the music, and when turned in the other, provided complete silence. It was then that I understood that picture and sound were not necessarily connected. Only years later did I appreciate what a tremendous advantage that was.

In the late '60s, when we used to sit around and talk about movies, one area that we would always emphasize was the sound. "Sound is 50 percent of the whole cinema experience," we would say. "It is your best friend, because it works on the audience secretly."

Yet everything in the movies seemed to favor the picture: The money was spent, by and large, on the picture and its visual elements—the sets, the costumes and the lighting. Sound was always given second place. We would patiently wait for hours as the photographer fiddled with the light, or the make-up artists adjusted a wig, while the soundman's modest request for a moment to find and shut off a refrigerator in the next apartment was always greeted with intolerance. Many times did I hear an unsympathetic photographer—who himself had used up two hours of precious time in preparation of a shot—fire back to the soundman, "You can't loop pictures!"

Yet the small group of ex-UCLA and USC filmmakers who had made the journey to San Francisco in order to be independent truly understood the parity of picture and sound. And we used our newly found independence to create the means for sound to take its rightful place beside picture. It was here that some of the most ambitious soundtracks in movies were attempted; here that the term "sound designer" was coined and used; here that the 24-track recorder was bridled and harnessed for film purposes; and it was also here that innovations in noise suppression and advanced quadrophonic theater presentation were born.

Perhaps these sound-for-picture sentiments are uncontested today. I think now filmmakers and audiences both understand and appreciate the unique importance and opportunities that the fully developed, modern, creative soundtrack can achieve. And of course, as with the cinema itself, there is no limit. We are still learning. —*Francis Ford Coppola*

© COLUMBIA PICTURES

vii

Foreword

SOUND FOR PICTURE

An Inside Look at Audio Production For Film and Television

FILM

The Art Of Soundtrack Design

How to Help Tell A Story With Sound

BY JOHN MICHAEL WEAVER

THE CREATION OF A MOTION PICTURE SOUNDTRACK is—or at least has the potential of being—an art as well as a craft. Especially within the context of narrative feature filmmaking, it is a process that involves a tremendous amount of selection, gathering and orchestration of individual sound elements, which must then be mixed together carefully to create a coherent whole.

When it comes to getting training in such a complex and creative discipline, *experience* may indeed be the best teacher. But how do you get the necessary experience in a business that, as veteran re-recording mixer Bill Varney points out, "doesn't give you much room for practice"?

Sound designer Walter Murch notes a further complication: "There is no 'way' to get into the film industry." That is, unlike many professions, there is no sanctioned training ground that necessarily provides an entry into the field. Each person must find his or her own opening, the proverbial "foot in the door."

Although having a diploma in hand certainly doesn't guarantee that the door will swing open any more easily, getting a thorough pre-professional education, which includes both a technical and aesthetic dimension, can be an important step toward your professional goals. Getting *through* the door is only part of the problem, however. What skills and abilities will you need to have once you're on the inside? How much of this can you learn in school?

These questions were posed to several prominent professionals: Ben Burtt (*Star Wars*, *Raiders of the Lost Ark*, *E.T.*); James G. Stewart (*Gunga Din*, *The Hunchback of Notre Dame*, *Citizen Kane*); Bill Varney (*The Black Stallion*, *Raiders of the Lost Ark*, *The Empire Strikes Back)*; and Walter Murch (*The Godfather*, *The Conversation*, *Apocalypse Now*). All have received Academy Awards for their work in film sound.

Storytelling, Creativity and Learning to Listen

First of all, the study of soundtrack design is essentially an inquiry into how to help tell a story with sound. If there is one thing the top people working in this field have in common, it is that they possess strong storytelling instincts. Ben Burtt says, "I think that any artist who participates in the filmmaking process—an artist who is going to get recognized as such—is one who appreciates the overall purpose of the movie. In other words, they're first and foremost supporters of the film as a total piece of drama, or whatever the goal of this film is. We love the movie, and we say, 'What can I do personally, with my own skills, to make this story better?' That's what appeals to us, that challenge."

Secondly, someone who aspires to make the kind of creative contribution Burtt refers to needs to possess technical expertise *and* an aesthetic point of view. Varney notes that a director "will often let you present a scene to them in whatever way you feel it's going to work, and then he or she makes the final decision."

At the same time, you shouldn't expect to be able to flex your artistic muscles on every project. James G. Stewart, one of Hollywood's most experienced and accomplished soundmen, says, "The opportunity for creativity doesn't present itself unless you have a producer or director who appreciates that sort of thing and understands it."

Walter Murch at work on
Apocalypse Now

Finally, as frustrating as it may be to those looking for easy answers, there are no formulas or universally accepted principles to rely on when it comes to making aesthetic choices. A student must realize that there is no single way to design a soundtrack. There are only *approaches* that work in different situations, at different times for different reasons. And this is what keeps the work interesting and challenging, Varney believes. Otherwise, "It wouldn't be a very creative process."

Thus, the intention of the following discussion is not to define the "correct" method of designing a soundtrack, but rather to make suggestions that might help a student develop his or her own ideas on the subject. Probably the best place to begin is to learn how to *listen*.

Sight, Sound and Perception

Before focusing your attention specifically on how movie soundtracks are conceived and structured, it is helpful to examine how humans tend to organize and process the sights and sounds of the real world. "Because of the priorities of the brain, the audio channels are suppressed relative to the visual channels," Murch explains. "We attend first to the visual, and then augment that with sound." However, this "supplementary" information can have a major effect on our experience of what we are seeing. That is, we tend to "see" things differently depending on what we hear at the same time. You can confirm this easily by walking down a city street wearing headphones and observing how your environment looks and feels, depending on which cassette you have in your Walkman.

It is also important to recognize that we generally don't pay equal attention to all of the auditory stimuli we are exposed to in our immediate environment. Depending on our mood, expectations and any number of other psychological and emotional variables, we ignore much of the acoustic energy that reaches our ears and, to a large extent, simply hear what is important to us at any given moment. To heighten awareness of just how complex our aural environment is and how much we filter out, Murch recommends that students "spend a lot of time with their eyes closed. If possible, put a blindfold on and walk around with a friend who'll make sure you don't get run over. That forces you to pay conscious attention to a whole universe

> We tend to "see" things differently depending on what we hear at the same time.

Ben Burtt

[of sound] that surrounds you all the time."

By doing this kind of exercise, you will become more aware of the rich palette of aural "colors" available when creating a soundtrack and of how to hear these sounds as separate entities, rather than an amorphous mass. Varney describes how these individual elements can be manipulated, depending on the desired effect: "We are painting a very special picture with sound, and we can alter the audience's experience of a scene simply by going with a different element, going with a different balance."

Listening to Movies

The next step is to begin studying the ways in which our expectations of how a film "should" sound differ from how we perceive sound in everyday life. "I think the sound designer has to be aware of how sound has been done historically," says Burtt, whose knowledge of the history of film sound seems encyclopedic. "Each person who comes into a movie has seen thousands of other movies, and you have to take that into account. That doesn't mean you have to copy, it just means that you have to know [about it]. I think the best education a new artist could have, in any field, is to learn all the way up to where the frontier is, and then take those few steps beyond it."

The difficulty is that despite our vast experience with *watching* films, we are not in the habit of consciously *listening* to them. The images on the screen are often so overwhelming that we remain relatively oblivious to the sounds accompanying them. It becomes necessary to find the means to direct our attention, at least temporarily, to the soundtrack alone.

One simple way this can be accomplished is by listening to a soundtrack without looking at the accompanying images. Switch off the lamp in the film projector, disconnect the video input to your monitor or simply close your eyes. Listen carefully, make a list of the individual sounds that you hear and try to imagine what the scene might look like. Also, try to discern what is going on, dramatically, within the scene. Then, replay the scene with the picture. Because you have broken down the track into its component parts, you can now more easily consider how they are arranged in relation to one another and in relation to the visuals.

The opposite approach is also instructive. Turn off the sound and just watch a scene before listening to it. Ask yourself, "If I were building up a soundtrack from nothing, what sounds would I include and what would I leave out? On what basis would I make those decisions?" Then listen to what the filmmakers actually did with the scene, and compare it to what you had in mind.

"Go to the art library and take out a book of paintings. Then go to the music library and try to choose music that stretches the point of a particular painting as far as it can be stretched." —Walter Murch

The Soundtrack as Art

Once students become better listeners, the soundtrack can be put back into context, and even more probing questions can be considered. Why were particular sounds selected or emphasized? What psychological or emotional effect is a particular use of sound intended to have on the audience? What are the filmmakers trying to communicate through sound?

Sometimes the answers to these questions are very uncomplicated. Often a door slam is *just* a door slam. But there are many instances in which a soundtrack is operating on more than one level. Burtt says, "You can do something in the soundtrack that on one hand may be sort of literal and has a meaning just within the naturalness of that scene, but on the other hand—if you've chosen the right sound—has a whole other meaning that comments on the scene as well." (See sidebar: "Designing a Scene.")

Motivating students to look for the intention or meaning behind a particular use of sound can be difficult at first. It's as though you were asking them to violate some unwritten taboo. This is "a tribute to the coercive power of film," Murch says. "A film has its own authority that seems to deny the fact that anyone was involved in it or made it happen."

Stewart, who trained numerous people to be re-recording mixers during his 50 years in the film industry, remembers how one group of students reacted when he introduced the subject of aesthetics: "When we started out, I didn't run picture or track. I talked to them about the relationship between what you see and what you hear in a film. I think they got a little impatient with me. They just wanted to get to it!"

Understanding the Complete "Picture"

Being eager to spring into action is a natural tendency, but deciding which approach is appropriate for a given scene is not simple. Don't despair—asking the right questions is half the battle. "What is the movie about at this point? What is the picture showing us? How should the soundtrack relate to that? It's not just the literal selection of sounds," Burtt maintains, "it's the selection of sounds in relationship to picture—picture that's just happened, that's about to happen, that's happening right now."

Stewart also stresses the importance of being aware of the "relationship between the visual and the aural" and having a sense of when a particular combination *works*. "I can't judge music, because I'm not a musician," he says, "but I do know when music fits with what's on the screen." Students need to develop an understanding of how *all* parts of a film relate to the whole.

Designing a Scene

Walter Murch talks about his own approach to the creative process of soundtrack design:

"You have to look at a scene and break it down into field [distant, diffuse, atmospheric sounds], midground and foreground, because you can't record everything all together. You can't record the footsteps with the jet planes in the right perspective at the same time. So, the first, most important step is to break down reality into layers that can be manipulated. Once you start thinking in layers, then you will know how to separate things out. Once they're separate, they are free-floating, and you can replace the obvious with the not-so-obvious.

"When you first think about a scene, your tendency is to be more literal. But the more you look at it from the side, rather than confronting it directly—once you have that 'lateral vision,' rather than 'literal vision'—you can come up with things that are very unlikely, yet you put them in and it seems to work. It works because, if it's a well-chosen sound, the audience (which includes yourself) responds to it, both because it does resonate with something that is going on inside the characters, and because it's reasonable that this sound would be there."

Murch describes a scene from *The Godfather* to illustrate this point: "Just before Michael kills McClusky and Sollotzo, by far the loudest thing on the soundtrack is this incredible screech, which is in no way explained by anything that you've seen up to that point. It happens to be the sound of an elevated train going around a corner, but we've never established that there are elevated trains [present], other than through sound. Yet, this wave of sound comes and goes and comes back and gets even louder, then gets eliminated as soon as he pulls the trigger. In a literal sense, maybe down the street there was an elevated train that we didn't see when we pulled up to this restaurant, but you really have to stretch the fabric to say, 'Okay, I'll buy that.' On the other hand, this sound very accurately described what was going on inside this kid's head as he was about to murder someone for the first time in his life, up close: the screeching and the raging of the brain. 'Should I do it? Should I do it? Yes! BANG!' "

Listen and Learn

There are literally hundreds of films worth listening to and studying. Here are just a few, and their directors:

2001: A Space Odyssey, Stanley Kubrick
A Clockwork Orange, Stanley Kubrick
Alexander Nevsky, Sergei Eisenstein
All That Jazz, Bob Fosse
American Graffiti, George Lucas
Apocalypse Now, Francis Ford Coppola
The Birds, Alfred Hitchcock
The Black Stallion, Caroll Ballard
Blow Out, Brian DePalma
Bonnie and Clyde, Arthur Penn
Citizen Kane, Orson Welles
Close Encounters of the Third Kind, Steven Spielberg
The Conversation, Francis Ford Coppola
Dodes'ka-den, Akira Kurosawa
Doctor Zhivago, David Lean
Frankenstein, James Whale
The Godfather, Francis Ford Coppola
The Graduate, Mike Nichols
Great Expectations, David Lean
King Kong, Merian C. Cooper & Ernest B. Schoedsack
La Grande Illusion, Jean Renoir
The Last Emperor, Bernardo Bertolucci
Lawrence of Arabia, David Lean
Little Big Man, Arthur Penn
M, Fritz Lang
The Magnificent Ambersons, Orson Welles
Monsieur Hulot's Holiday, Jacques Tati
Nashville, Robert Altman
Psycho, Alfred Hitchcock
Raging Bull, Martin Scorsese
Raiders of the Lost Ark, Steven Spielberg
The Servant, Joseph Losey
Star Wars, George Lucas
Taxi Driver, Martin Scorsese
Wild Strawberries, Ingmar Bergman
Wings of Desire, Wim Wenders

Murch suggests an interesting way to explore the relationship between sound and image: "Go to the art library and take out a book of paintings. Then go to the music library and try to choose music that stretches the point of a particular painting as far as it can be stretched." Murch uses impressionist painter Edgar Degas' *L'Absinthe*, a picture of two dejected-looking people sitting in a cafe, as an example. "You say, 'What is this picture about?' and if it's the vacant expression on this poor woman's face, then choose music that gets at that, rather than the fact that she's in a cafe." By doing this type of exercise, Murch says, you begin learning how to "get at a feeling that is neither in the picture nor in the soundtrack, but is the result of a synthesis of the two, which is what it's really all about."

Education and Beyond

Learning to interpret the dramatic requirements of a film and design a soundtrack that meets those needs takes a great deal of time, patience and practice. Therefore, another essential part of a student's education is getting hands-on experience using sound as a storytelling tool. Exercises that provide this kind of training include putting together a simple story using sound alone (such as a short radio play or audio documentary); creating an entirely new soundtrack for an existing scene from a movie or television show; and, best of all, designing a soundtrack for a student film. The opportunity to experiment and work on projects with other students who share an interest in exploring sound's creative potential is one of the most productive aspects of being in school.

What happens when you leave school and begin to pursue a career in film sound depends entirely on the individual. "It's a little bit like Alice looking at the mirror," says Murch. "By the power of her imagination, she found herself on the other side of the mirror. I think all of us who work in film have gone through something like that kind of experience. And it's good that we do, because what happens when you're inside this fairyland is that you're endlessly faced with a series of mirrors and walls. And by some effort of will, imagination, persistence or luck, you have to continue to get through these." Regardless of how good your preliminary education has been, it is necessary to maintain an open and flexible attitude, because mastering any art form is a *very* long-term proposition.◐

Sounding Off in A Visual Medium

WHEN WALTER MURCH AND BEN BURTT brought the title "sound designer" into feature films in the late 1970s, they couldn't have foreseen the size of the hornet's nest they were kicking. In a business well-known for wacky, ambiguous and grandiose job descriptions, this particular credit has generated more than its share of blank stares, shouting matches and quite a few chuckles. Most of us who have received the credit on feature films feel a little uneasy about it ourselves.

It's hard to explain why the words "sound designer" seem pretentious. But they somehow do. Clearly, the word "designer" is the provocative one. A designer is someone who imagines, organizes and so on. No problem so far. Some of the queasiness about the use of the word "design" in connection with "sound" must stem from the notion that we who request that credit place ourselves above all the others—that we believe we are doing something new or more sophisticated than what has been done before. Or maybe it just seems pretentious to imply that any one person would have the expertise to understand every aspect of the planning, fabricating, collecting and processing of sound in a film.

As to whether a sound designer is doing anything new, the answer is emphatically "No and Yes." The Yes part (which is not as important as the No part) has a lot to do with technology.

By the early '70s, pop music recording technology began to creep into film sound. And as new gadgets began appearing in movie post-production sound (most notably the multitrack tape recorder), so did a new style of working. Individuals who had experience with music studio gear—and who could get some help linking the picture and audio via SMPTE time code—could record, edit, process and mix much of the sound by themselves. Each of those jobs previously had been done by a specialist. But this new, completely unspecialized approach to the work was not immediately accepted in Los Angeles because of the precise and strictly enforced classification of jobs by the unions. Enter San Francisco, wild and woolly as usual.

Francis Coppola and George Lucas moved to the Bay Area in the late 1960s. They were young renegades, inclined toward experimenting with new ways to make movies. Very little might have come of all this experimenting if they hadn't made some outstanding films, which happened to have truly extraordinary soundtracks. *The Conversation*, *American Graffiti*, *Star Wars*, *Apocalypse Now*, *The Black Stallion* and *Raiders of the Lost Ark*

Confessions of An Occasional Sound Designer

BY RANDY THOM

Francis Coppola and George Lucas were young renegades, inclined toward experimenting with new ways to make movies. Very little might have come of all of this experimenting if they hadn't made some outstanding films that happened to have truly extraordinary soundtracks.

all broke new ground in terms of sound and captured the attention of The Industry down south. (*Star Wars*, *Raiders* and *The Black Stallion* were mixed in Los Angeles, where the first two were partially edited, but Ben Burtt and Alan Splet did most of their sound design work in Northern California.)

The high quality and innovation apparent in these film soundtracks is sometimes attributed to the fact that most of them had post-production schedules significantly longer than those typical in Hollywood. I don't find this argument very compelling because we can all think of films with very long periods of post-production that did not result in groundbreaking soundtracks. I also am not convinced that the unspecialized style or the new gadgets used on these Northern California films are what made sound such a powerful part of their dramatic impact.

Does using a digital audio workstation make you a sound designer? There are plenty of films these days for which an individual has recorded, edited, processed and premixed a few of the sounds that wind up being used. If creating a spaceship sound by using digital processing constitutes sound design, then creating a spaceship sound by altering speed and equalization in the analog domain (as was done many times in the 1950s) was surely sound design as well. Should you get the credit "sound designer" if you only create three or four sound effects in a two-hour film? Probably not.

Apocalypse Now is often cited as an example of great film sound design, and it was the first time that most of us saw the title sound designer. Walter Murch, who was in charge of the sound for that film, was also one of its principal picture editors, just as he had been on *The Conversation*.

After Murch received the sound design credit the genie was out of the bottle. Burtt got his first sound design credit soon afterward for *More American Graffiti*. Splet, creating powerful sound montages for films by David Lynch and Carroll Ballard, would soon adopt the title as well.

When Murch fabricated, processed, edited and mixed much of the sound on the early Zoetrope projects, the new generation of equipment he used came to be associated with the title he chose for himself on *Apocalypse*. Today the list of exotic, computer-based tools is expanding so fast that nobody can keep up with it. And the term sound designer continues to be linked with the use of weird and wonderful devices. On the rare occasion that sound designers are mentioned in the popular press, they are often referred to as "wizards," evoking the image of strange hermits who tinker in isolated laboratories with potions and obscure, complex machines. This image is unfortunate to the degree that it stresses isolation. The power of sound artists and of their work grows out of collaboration, not isolation. And the usefulness of sound to a film and to the film community is proportional to its comprehensibility to collaborators in other crafts. Directors who don't understand sound, at least on an intuitive level, are in no position to use it.

What is *not* new about designing sound is the part of the job that depends on the brain and the heart. And it is a much more important element than the technology. Anyone who devises a particular sound aesthetic for a

movie and supervises the implementation of that approach has designed the sound. Using this definition, sound design has been done for generations. What difference does it make whether the tools are a Nagra and an upright Moviola or a DAT and a digital audio workstation?

It's strange that film composers haven't been more vocal about the proliferation of the sound designer title. They are obviously in the business of designing sound and might be justified in feeling their turf invaded. But the class structure of the movie business is set up so that composers are the one group in the craft of sound whose work is occasionally given the same kind of respect as that of the "major" crafts: acting, directing, photography, writing. Movie composers don't need to bother themselves much about this new credit called "sound design," because they're paid enough and given enough respect to be safely above what might seem to them an amusing sideshow.

So it's the production mixers, re-recording mixers and supervising sound editors who usually lead the opposition to those who call themselves sound designers. As usual, the most vicious fights are over the scraps, not the entree, which leads me finally to the underlying and much more important issue.

Quite simply, sound is not taken seriously by most filmmakers. This unfortunate idea that sound is of secondary importance stole its way not only into the consciousness of filmmakers but, more incredibly, into the film sound community itself. We in sound have been told for so long that our labor is of secondary importance in the grand scheme of filmmaking that we have actually come to believe it. So even if we know that our creative work on a particular project has been crucial to the dramatic impact of the movie, we don't dare ask for credit at the beginning of the film or be brazen

Star Wars is one of the influential films that has high-quality, innovative sound design.

Sound design has been done for generations. What difference does it make whether the tools are a Nagra and an upright Moviola or a DAT and a digital audio workstation?

enough to claim we "designed" anything. We are, according to the official code, only "technicians."

Instead of collaborating with directors, writers and editors to explore the enormous potential of sound in film, we spend most of our time dealing with sound in the most obvious, remedial and banal ways. We buy into the notion that sound is an afterthought in the filmmaking process, with the side effect of resentment toward our peers who seem brash and assertive.

What does it mean to take sound seriously? Most importantly, it means being interested in exploring the storytelling capacity of sound, from the writing of the script through production and post-production. It means more than simply recording sound effects on location, but also considering the ways those sounds can be used to make the characters and locations in the film more compelling. It means searching for connections that sound can make between places, characters and moments within the film, and between the film and the culture at large. It means not being so quick to put sound effects and music into separate and unequal pigeonholes. It means not being reluctant to let the visual images follow and complement the sound. It means finding ways to shoot and structure the film that will open the door to the collaboration of sound. And ultimately, it means encouraging sound to influence creative decisions in the other crafts.

Walter Murch

The most powerful moments in film tend to be those where some degree of ambiguity in the visual presentation causes the audience to unconsciously look for other clues to complete the story. The sequences in movies that use sound best are often the ones that have been shot using slow motion, odd p.o.v.'s, dim light, unusual visual superimpositions, black-and-white images, or transitions into and out of dreams or hallucinations. One example is *Backdraft*, for which Gary Rydstrom helped make the fire a living character by weaving creature sounds behind the strange, slow motion images of flame. Another is *Barton Fink*, where idiosyncratic, dream-like visuals open the door to Skip Lievsay's evocative sounds.

Similarly, the hyper-real, super-amplified vision of action-adventure films takes us into a different set of worlds, providing another set of ambiguities for our senses to reconcile and other opportunities for sound to provide clues. In this sound genre nobody has done better than Ben Burtt, whose sound ideas, every bit as much as John Williams' music, made the *Star Wars* and *Indiana Jones* films sing with excitement.

Another element common to films that use sound effectively is the presence in the story of a listener: a perceiver of events, a strong, well-defined point of view through which we, the audience, vicariously experience the action. In *Apocalypse Now* it is Captain Willard; in *The Black Stallion* it is the boy Alec. In *Raging Bull* Jake Lamotta suffers Sugar Ray's slow-motion steamroller punches for us. The visual images and the dialog or lack of it usually must establish and support a strong p.o.v. in order for sound to be an effective contributor. Ironically, it is often the calculated use of ambiguity or distortion in the visual and verbal presentation that best sets up such a p.o.v. Too often the only role sound is allowed to play is its most obvious one, that of supporting reality. "See a dog, hear a dog" is the way it is usually described. Disguising the contrivance of the filmmaking process is certainly one of sound's jobs, but to ignore all of its other talents is a tragedy.

I endorse the "holistic" approach to filmmaking in which the movie is seen not as a collection of isolated crafts but as a complex collaboration among them. I realize that I'm not exactly breaking new aesthetic ground here, and none of this is really news to a lot of people in The Industry. When things are going well in moviemaking, the various crafts tend to disappear into each other, and their individual contributions to the finished film are difficult even for professionals to identify and analyze.

Francis Ford Coppola and friend during the filming of *Bram Stoker's Dracula*

Earlier I mentioned that Walter Murch received two credits on *Apocalypse Now*: picture editor and sound designer. The reason the movie employed sound so powerfully is not simply that Murch was a wizard at finding neat sounds to accompany a predetermined sequence of visual images and words. The first reel of *Apocalypse Now* was edited by Murch and directed by Coppola, using music, sound effects and visual images as equal components. They employed the same approach on *The Conversation*. Sometimes the music determined what shot would be chosen, sometimes the sound effects; sometimes the visuals led, sometimes dialog. The elements were mutually dependent, and there was a willingness to experiment in order to find what worked best. For once, the picture editing and sound editing departments were not cast in the role of mutual antagonists. Rather, they were free to give each other ideas.

The fact that the audience isn't usually aware of the power of sound is both a blessing and a curse to those who work the machinery aimed at the ear. The sound is, after all, invisible, which allows it to sneak through the side door to the brain. But that which is invisible rarely gets the credit (or the blame) it deserves.

Not every film needs precisely manicured, innovative or highly stylized sound to be successful. But many do require something special in terms of sound, and countless others could benefit from it enormously. It is hard for me to imagine *Raging Bull* without Frank Warner's wonderfully stylized effects, *Eraserhead* without the work of Alan Splet, *Rumblefish* without Richard Beggs' contribution, *The Conversation* without Walter Murch's sound imagination, or *Star Wars* without Ben Burtt. What sets the best soundtracks apart from the others is not budget, schedule, the latest gadgets or even genius itself. It is simply the fact that someone was thinking seriously about the collaborative ways that sound and image could be used from the earliest stages of the filmmaking process. This sort of approach certainly isn't a guarantee of great sound, but it is a necessary condition for great sound, and it is what sound design is all about.⌣

James G. Stewart

WHEN JAMES G. STEWART arrived in Hollywood in the late 1920s, the "talking picture" was still in its infancy. During the 50 years that followed, he remained consistently on the forefront of the technical and artistic advances made in film and television sound. Retracing the course of his career reveals a great deal not only about Stewart's personal accomplishments, which include nine Academy Award nominations and three Oscars, but also about how audio post-production evolved from a shaky new craft into the complex and sophisticated process it is today.

Getting in on the Ground Floor

Stewart's first love was radio. In 1920, at the age of 13, he participated in the experimental AM broadcasts conducted by Westinghouse engineer Frank Conrad that led to the setting up of KDKA Pittsburgh, America's first commercial radio station. When he was just out of high school, Stewart started his own radio repair business the same year that Warner Bros. released its first Vitaphone (sound-on-disc) feature, *Don Juan* (1926).

Two years later, Stewart's technical expertise and knowledge of sound reproduction helped him land a job in New York with the newly formed RCA Photophone Company, manufacturers of film sound recording and playback systems. While working for RCA, he designed, installed and maintained some of the first sound systems put in movie theaters, including the Radio City Music Hall theater, one of the largest cinemas ever built.

Stewart's first job in a Hollywood studio was with RKO (then owned by RCA), which hired him in 1931 to help develop a noise reduction system for the company's optical recording equipment. When the studio decided shortly thereafter that this type of research was a luxury it couldn't afford, Stewart was transferred to the production side of the operation and worked as a "stage man" (boom operator) on many early sound film classics, among them George Cukor's *A Bill of Divorcement* (1932), Katherine Hepburn's film debut.

"You had big crews in those days, six or seven people just for sound," Stewart recalls. "You had a mixer in a booth, a stage man, maybe two sound electricians and two sound grips. When we went on location, half of the time I didn't even know everyone on the sound crew." Stewart also points out that for a short time during the early days of Hollywood's conversion to sound, the production mixer's power on the set sometimes rivaled the director's. Recordists were able to insist that cameras be isolated in soundproof booths, and they even had the authority to cut a scene-in-progress when they didn't like what they were hearing.

The results were not always pleasing. "If you *look* at pictures made in the first year after sound was introduced, they have a static quality that's terrible," Stewart says. It wasn't long before directors rebelled against the artistic restrictions being foisted on them. "The demands the creative

Post-Production Pioneer

BY JOHN MICHAEL WEAVER

James G. Stewart's career in film sound spanned the first 50 years of the medium's history.

people put on the sound technicians [brought about] improvements in both recording technique and equipment, such as directional microphones and better booms."

From the Desert to Dubbing

Stewart's move into post-production was partially the consequence of a sunstroke he suffered in 1933 while on location in the Yuma Desert, where he was recording production sound for John Ford's *The Lost Patrol*. While recuperating back in Hollywood, he was asked to sit in on some "dubbing" (re-recording) sessions at RKO and write a report on what he observed.

"In the early days, re-recording was a process you indulged in only if it was absolutely necessary," Stewart says. "The release track on most pictures was 80 to 90 percent unaltered original sound." Whenever re-recording was deemed unavoidable, only specific sections of a reel would be worked on and later intercut with the production track.

At first, RKO productions were re-recorded using equipment originally designed for other purposes and under working conditions that were far from ideal. Individual optical tracks were played back on modified film projectors and were combined via the same extremely simple consoles used for mixing production sound. RKO's original dubbing room was a cramped, un-ventilated booth in which the mixer watched the film through a window and listened to the soundtrack through a small speaker mounted on the wall *behind* the console.

As primitive as this sounds by today's standards, the biggest problem was not the equipment or facilities but the way mixing was approached conceptually. The process was mostly handled by people from the music department. "They would make three or four takes of a reel, each one with the music a little louder, and then print them all," Stewart remembers. "The next day they would listen to them and maybe the music was a little too loud, even in the softest one. So they would have to go back and do more takes."

Stewart believed that with more rehearsal and less emphasis on music alone, it would be possible to do fewer takes and then intercut between them when necessary. After reading his report, RKO put him in charge of the studio's re-recording operations. During his tenure as chief re-recording mixer (1933-1945), he was at the console for nearly 250 films, including such classics as *Bringing Up Baby*, *Gunga Din*, *The Hunchback of Notre Dame*, the Marx Brothers' *Room Service* and almost all of the Fred Astaire and Ginger Rogers musicals. He also played a key role in many technical milestones reached at RKO, such as the making of the first three-strip Technicolor feature, Rouben Mamoulian's *Becky Sharp* (1935), and the introduction of electronic compression to the post-production process.

The first experiments at RKO with compression, conducted in the mid-1930s, were instigated by an executive who thought that an "automatic volume control" might be able to replace mixers altogether. Although this dubious scheme was quickly abandoned, Stewart and his assistant, Terry Kellum, discovered that compression actually did help solve a major technical problem that RKO and many other studios had with RCA's variable-area optical recording equipment.

> "You had big crews in those days, six or seven people just for sound. You had a mixer in a booth, a stage man, maybe two sound electricians and two sound grips. When we went on location, half of the time I didn't even know everyone on the sound crew."—James G. Stewart

"Theoretically," Stewart says, "area track was much better than [variable density, the competing format]. In practice, it flunked. It had tremendous range, but it was loaded with distortion. When we inserted compression circuitry into the re-recording chain, we got much better results." Not long after Stewart reported his findings to his superiors, the studio's parent company, RCA, began manufacturing a compressor designed specifically for re-recording.

"This device was absolutely revolutionary," says Stewart. "Now you could produce a track that was low in distortion and had at least 8 to 10 dB more gain. It caught on right away." By demonstrating and writing about the effect of compression on variable-area recordings, Stewart was instrumental in securing the format's widespread acceptance and long-term viability.

Making History with Welles

Stewart is probably best known for his work on Orson Welles' *Citizen Kane* (1941), regarded by many as one of the greatest films ever made. Although Stewart collaborated with many legendary directors during his career, including Frank Capra, George Cukor, Howard Hawks, Alfred Hitchcock, Fritz Lang and Jean Renoir, his association with Welles remains a high point. Welles had already established a name for himself with his original and flamboyant theater and radio productions. "He came to the motion-picture business totally sound-minded," Stewart says. "I don't know of any person I worked with who understood the soundtrack better."

Citizen Kane was the 25-year-old Welles' first major film, yet it is still studied today as a visual and aural masterpiece. "There is so much innovation in *Citizen Kane*," Stewart says, "because Orson had complete control over the picture—nobody interfered with him, whatever he wanted to do.

He didn't believe in any of the conventional things that stop imagination. He also had a cameraman and a soundman who were wide-open to suggestion. Whatever Orson dreamed up, we tried to do. I learned a great deal from him that I was able to apply later in my career."

James G. Stewart (left) and Terry Kellum seated at the RCA console that Stewart helped design for RKO's re-recording stage (circa 1937)

Stewart illustrates the nature of his working relationship with Welles by describing how the soundtrack for the famous Madison Square Garden scene in *Citizen Kane* was created. In the completed film, Kane, played by Welles, appears to be giving a political speech in an enormous auditorium. In fact, most of what we see of "the audience" and "the hall" is actually the work of a matte painter. Stewart's job was to make Welles sound as if he really were speaking before thousands of people in a huge, reverberant space.

Stewart says that Welles usually allowed him to work on a scene independently and would critique what he had done after it was finished. In this case, Welles had laid the groundwork by saying his lines in the slow, deliberate way a skilled orator would in a highly reflective environment. This inspired Stewart to not only add diffuse artificial reverberation (via RKO's acoustic echo chamber), but also to synthesize the kind of distinct echoes one would expect to hear in such a setting. He accomplished this by having additional prints of the original dialog track made and then offsetting those copies by varying amounts to create multiple repeats of Welles' words.

"I did the most elaborate track you can imagine," Stewart says, "but when I ran it for Orson, he said, 'Jimmy, with all that in there, who in the hell is going to listen to me?'" Despite all the time and effort Stewart had invested, he saw Welles' point immediately and proceeded to rebalance the mix so that the effects enhanced rather than dominated the scene.

Surrounding Selznick

Stewart left RKO in 1945 to work for David O. Selznick, producer of epic films like *Gone With the Wind*. Stewart was eventually named head of all technical operations for the producer's independent production company. Selznick's penchant for spectacle allowed Stewart to experiment with an early version of "surround sound" in the 1948 release *Portrait of Jennie*, a romantic fantasy about eternal love that culminates in a spectacular, surrealistic hurricane sequence. Ironically, even though the film earned Stewart an Academy Award for Best Special Sound Effects, very few people saw or heard the most audacious version of its finale.

Selznick wanted to dramatically increase the image size for the climactic storm scene, and Stewart followed suit by augmenting the main soundtrack by means of a separate surround channel. "For the preview in Oakland, I recorded a special track that had nothing on it except wind and waves," recalls Stewart. "In addition to the regular speakers behind the screen, we put six more speakers around the room, three on each side. I had two gain controls, one for the main speakers and one for the side speakers, so I was able to open up the 'storm track' as the picture increased in size on the screen.

"On the way out of the theater, without asking me anything about how it was done, Selznick said, 'Jimmy, I want a hundred of those!'" Unfortu-

James G. Stewart (far left, partial view) with Orson Welles (standing, right) and others at the RCA console in RKO's re-recording stage (early 1940s)

nately, logistical and financial realities prevented anyone other than preview audiences from experiencing the film's ending as Selznick and Stewart had envisioned it.

The Television Age

In 1950, Stewart moved to yet another innovative organization, Glen Glenn Sound, where he remained for nearly 25 years. During this period of radical transformation in Hollywood, Glen Glenn was often in the vanguard of technological change, laying claim to the introduction of such breakthroughs as synchronous 1/4-inch magnetic tape recorders, ADR and reversal re-recording.

Glen Glenn also made an early entry into the fledgling TV market. Stewart's previous experience at RKO mixing hundreds of inexpensive, tightly scheduled B-pictures proved to be the ideal preparation for working within the time and budgetary constraints of television. "At RKO, I used to figure that to mix a reel a day on an A-picture [about ten minutes of screen time] was a pretty good job," recalls Stewart. "But on a B-picture we did three reels a day. Later, when I was doing TV, I mixed two complete shows a day, three reels per show." Thus, while he continued to do some feature films, the bulk of Stewart's time at Glenn was spent mixing the numerous TV productions posted there, among them *The Jack Benny Show*, *The Real McCoys*, *The Andy Griffith Show* and *I Love Lucy*.

It was the advent of reversal re-recording techniques in the 1960s that made it easier to sustain the grueling pace demanded by television production schedules. Before "rock and roll" transport systems and punch-in recording were developed, an entire reel had to be mixed in real time. If any portion of the mix was unacceptable, the whole thing had to be redone. Once it became feasible to stop, roll back to any point on a reel and begin recording again from there, the necessity of multiple retakes was eliminated.

As often happens, though, the validity and value of this new technique was not immediately recognized by many in the industry used to working in the traditional way. "There was a lot of sophistry about not interrupting the 'dramatic flow' of the reel," Stewart says. "But mixing six reels was a normal day in television, which is almost impossible if you have to go back to the beginning of a reel and start over again every time somebody makes a mistake."

A Half-Century of Hindsight

In the mid-'70s, Stewart went to work for the studio that had ushered in the sound era nearly 50 years before, Warner Bros., and stayed there until he retired in 1980. Today, he looks back with both pride and some misgivings on how the post-production process has changed since the days when "talkies" were deemed by some to be a fad that wouldn't last.

Stewart feels that sound has not changed much from an artistic standpoint. "For the most part, people do many of the same things now as we did in the early days, but they do them faster and meet higher technical standards." Ben Burtt (*Star Wars*, *Raiders of the Lost Ark*), a prominent member of another generation of audio trailblazers, acknowledges that people like Stewart discovered the creative potential of sound: "We rediscovered it [in the '70s and '80s] with portable tape recorders and other electronic equipment that wasn't available to previous artists."

Stewart believes that one of the most significant changes to occur during his career was the gradual fragmentation and compartmentalization of the filmmaking process. When he first came to Hollywood, almost every phase of a project was handled in-house, and there was a great deal of creative collaboration between everyone working on a film. As the old studio system disintegrated, the people working on various facets of a production became increasingly isolated from one another.

"Today, the people who are actually sitting at the re-recording console with their hands on the knobs often have never seen the picture [they are mixing] before," Stewart says. "In many instances, they become merely an extension of the hands of the director. In the early days, I saw a film many times, in various stages of completion, before it came to the re-recording stage. It is much better if the people responsible for the soundtrack are in on a picture from its conception to its completion, so that they and the director can discuss things like motivation and pattern."

Staying Power

Having worked for so many years in such a demanding and volatile profession, how does Stewart account for the fact that he and his work have been able to stand the test of time?

He believes that one of his most valuable assets, particularly in the beginning, was his strong technical background. This enabled him to understand and explain to the people he worked with the capabilities and limita-

> "Orson Welles came to the motion-picture business totally sound-minded. I don't know of any person I worked with who understood the soundtrack better."—James G. Stewart

tions of the available tools. Equally important was his appreciation of the dramatic function of both the aural and visual elements within a film. This insight made it possible for him not only to interpret and execute the concepts of others, but also to contribute ideas of his own. In addition, his ability to adapt to different situations, combined with an eagerness to experiment, made him equally comfortable with a few hours to re-record a TV show, a few days to mix a B-film or a few weeks to perfect a complex soundtrack.

Although Stewart is no longer professionally active, his effect on the sound of American film and television continues. A large number of the films and shows he worked on can still be seen and heard on television, in revival theaters and in college classrooms. His presence can also be felt in the soundtracks created today by the many audio post-production specialists who have been influenced, either directly or indirectly, by the legacy of professionalism and artistry that Stewart established during his long and distinguished career.

What's That Sound?

It Takes Big Work To Make Even The Smallest Movie Sound Effect

BY BLAIR JACKSON

P LUNGERS. TOILET PLUNGERS. For some reason that's not the answer I expected when I asked sound effects specialist and Foley mixer Greg Orloff how he created the sound of galloping horses for the film *Back to the Future III*. "Gee," I said, "why not just use coconuts like the 'horses' in *Monty Python & the Holy Grail*?"

"Oh, coconuts are pretty good, too," was his deadpan reply.

When I started this story, I thought it was going to be about sound wizards using samplers and digital workstations in conjunction with the latest outboard whiz-bangs to make incredible sci-fi noises. And I suppose those elements are here to a degree. But more than that, this is a tale of the incredible amount of work that goes into creating sound effects that, as viewers, we probably take for granted. What? You mean you're surprised that it took *eight days* to work up the sound for RoboCop's legs?

Yes, we're talking obsessive pursuit of perfection here. But the bottom line is that sound effects work is a craft, not just a job, and the people who work in the field are there because they love it. They'd better, because the hours are lousy, the pressure's intense and there's always the chance that the sound they slaved over for days on end will be buried under some overzealous composer's drippy score. Would you or I ever know if the gunshots in the Civil War film *Glory* were taken off a sound effects record of World War II battle noises? Probably not. But Lon Bender, whose job it was to come up with those Civil War gunshots, got into it—deeply into it—and so we sit in a darkened theater, wincing at every musket report, thinking, "Holy shit, this probably *is* what it was like!" That's the sound designer's art: the creation of a convincing reality—even if it's all just smoke and mirrors...or plungers and samplers.

One more thing. Sound effects people are listed under a hundred different titles in film credits: sound designer, special effects supervisor, supervising sound editor, you name it. There are shades of differences in those, but none of them really tell the story. I like Mark Mangini's tongue-in-cheek description of his job: "sound swami."

Horsing Around with Greg Orloff

A lthough the past decade or so has seen a move toward the use of increasingly sophisticated technologies in sound effects work, the Foley stage, with its "actors" tapping real footsteps or slamming car doors or breaking panes of glass, remains a vital part of the filmmaking process. Until he went to work for Lucasfilm, Greg Orloff was a principal Foley player/editor at Taj Filmworks in Los Angeles. Taj's credits include such mega-budget features as *The Abyss*, *The Little Mermaid*, *Back to the Future II* and *III*, *Young Guns II* and *Die Hard II*. (Lawdy, what would Hollywood do without sequels?) Orloff talked about the process of dubbing horse gallops for *Back to the Future III*, much of which takes place in the Old West.

Alan Howarth spent eight days developing the sound for RoboCop's legs.

"In a way, *Back to the Future* was like four shows in one for us. It was human footsteps, human props, all the horses and whatever they pull—stagecoaches and things like that—and then the futuristic machines. A lot of that was done in Foley.

"I think most of the time you hear horses in a film you're probably hearing something created in Foley," he continues. "We like to use plungers on different types of surfaces. The advantage of this method is that you can actually do it to sync instead of having an editor cut in each individual horse footstep. To get a large group of horses, you usually need at least five or six channels just for the group, and then you might augment that with thundering horses [from sound effects libraries] and any specific horses that jump out. We've used up to 20 channels just for the horses and their equipment. You try to get different ranges. If it's a cavalry charge or a stampede, you try to get a lot of low rumbling stuff. In streets, the foreground horses might be low and the background horses high, with more of a clip-clop sound. So that affects which surface you clop on and maybe what you're clopping with. Occasionally an editor has picked out specific horses you need to cover

"I think most of the time you hear horses in a film you're probably hearing something created in Foley." —Greg Orloff

Greg Orloff

in addition to the group, so you work up something that lets that horse stand out a little more. Microphone perspective and equalization comes into it, too. I try to mic differently for each visual perspective; I've never felt this could be done on fader alone.

"So that's what we try to do for everything we record, whether it's with props or whatever. For the horses in *Back to the Future III*, I used mainly Neumann KMR-82s.

"Sometimes we might do a mix for a temp dub, but we generally transfer it singly so [the editors] have as much control as possible later. They're working with an amazing amount of material: *Roger Rabbit* was 40 tracks of Foley per reel, as was *Die Hard II*. A lot of the major action films seem to be about 40 channels per reel just for Foley. Then there might be anywhere from 40 to 120 channels of sound effects in a reel.

"With something like the horses, the sound editor usually tries to treat them as a single track, then cut them to whatever other sound effects and Foley and dialog there are. Chuck Campbell had that job [on *Back to the Future III*], and he'd probably be the first to tell you it's a monumental task."

The Many Voices of Mark Mangini

Mark Mangini is one of several sound effects aces—including Steve Flick and Richard Anderson—who make up Weddington Productions of North Hollywood. Widely regarded as one of the top sound houses anywhere, the Weddington group snares work on many of the big Hollywood films each year—*RoboCop 2*, *Total Recall*, *The Exorcist* and *Gremlins II* are just a few of the movies transformed by the company's sound designers. Mangini shares some of the techniques he used to make the gremlins sound as weird and nasty as they do.

Mark Mangini

"I created all the gremlin voices for *Gremlins II*," he says. "That was one of my specific tasks. I did the original *Gremlins*, also. Actually, this particular job didn't require too much in the way of nifty gadgets. Most of it involved altering voices. So we had an ADR studio—actually Paramount's Stage L, their looping stage—modified so that a film projector could run varispeeded in interlock with a film recorder. Frequently, when the [gremlin] puppets are filmed, they're undercranked, so later you get this speeded up action; trying to lip sync to these guys at 24 frames a second is difficult for the actors. So we slow down the projector and interlock it with the recorder so it's easier to lip sync to. That also means that when we come back up to sync speed, the voice has a slightly speeded up, chipmunk effect. We can varispeed the projector to taste, to suit different variations.

"Then there was a whole variety of specialty gremlin voices that were done from those original recordings. The making of the gremlin voices was partially actors reading lines and making noises and things, speeded up later, and some of them were processed with some electronic outboard gear and then augmented with animal recordings.

"We made a bat gremlin that was interesting and fairly complex. I did some sampling, but most of it was done as live performance or with conventional editing techniques. I put together this rack of samplers and a mixer and a sequencer that I call 'The Rack of Doom,' and I brought it to the stage. It consists of two Roland S-550 samplers, a little 16-input rack-mounted mix console, some rack-mounted reverb devices—SPX90-type things—a MIDI-to-SMPTE interface and a Macintosh computer with Performer [Mark of the Unicorn's MIDI sequencer]. I've adapted Performer to allow me to work with it in 'feet' and 'frames,' which is not a function it normally has; I've managed to convert 'bars' and 'beats per minute' into 'feet' and 'frames.'

"I presampled a ton of sound effects. I basically created a sample library of sound effects and gremlin voices, and as we'd be mixing, the director would inevitably say, 'Gee, we need this here,' and it wasn't something we'd anticipated in sound effects editing. Since I had the sample library, it allowed me to load something quickly, lock it to picture, perform it to picture and give the director not just a sound, but the ability to massage it. You can spread it across a keyboard, play it around, process it a million different ways, and basically sound design on the spot. It turned out to be very efficient, and it really pleased everyone because we had sound effects at our beck and call, whereas in the past you'd have to go to the back room and loop or call back to the shop and get something transferred to mag, get it cut and wait hours for it.

"If there was a sound effect we didn't have on disk or mag, we could record it live directly into a sampler, frequently doing it vocally. We did dozens of effects that way to augment things. We did squishes, pops, drips and even gremlin voices on the spot. We'd sample it, then trigger it locked to picture.

"So the Rack of Doom actually functioned as a 'wild recorder'—a lot of soundstages have one. When we're dubbing, we use up our usual allotment of three recorders to create our dialog, music and effects stems, so you don't have an extra recorder when you're there on the spot. The samplers functioned as our wild recorder and allowed us to sample things, save them on disk and give them address points so they could be used easily later."

Lon Bender

Lon Bender's High-Tech Civil War

Glory won an Oscar for sound, and if you saw the film, no doubt you too were astounded by how real those gunshots and cannon blasts sounded. How were they done? I called Lon Bender of Soundelux in Hollywood to find out.

"Some of the most interesting things we did on *Glory* were the bullet whizzes and the incoming cannon balls," Bender says. "For the bullet whizzes, we had about 30 Civil War re-enactors come up to my ranch in Frazier Park [near L.A.] to record gunfire. We actually wanted to get the sound of real Civil War bullets being shot through the air, because we knew the velocity would not be the same as an M-16 or an AK-47; it would be slow enough to actually make an air whiz-by. So one of our guys got down-range in a gully about 400 yards away, and we shot live rounds at him—or at least near him. That's how we recorded them, and they were very, very effective. We used a DAT machine with a Neumann single-point stereo mic. The sounds were easily isolated, so then we put them on the Synclavier and that gave us a lot of flexibility in terms of how we could use the sound.

"We also went to Mississippi to record cannon balls. There we had a couple of DAT recorders set along a road on a private ranch 250 yards downrange and a quarter-mile downrange. I wanted the recorders to be far enough downrange that the initial explosion wouldn't contaminate the sound of the actual projectile going by. It's a matter of milliseconds, but it's important. This was wild—the re-enactors made up 50 real cannon balls out of iron. These guys are hardcore—they make their own cannons, too, actually forge them. Anyway, from a whole day of shooting these things off we only got one recording of a cannon ball whiz-by, because you couldn't aim them very well. That's the price you pay for having realistic cannons, I guess. In the end we discovered that when the bullet whiz-bys were manipulated—played in reverse on the Synclavier and slowed down—they sounded like the cannon ball whiz-bys we spent a whole day trying to record.

Alan Howarth

"Once we had what we wanted, we worked very hard to make the barrages interesting in the actual film, panning back and forth, working with levels and placement so it wasn't static. We cut on an AMS AudioFile, and I think there were upward of 200 tracks of just guns and weapons. The great thing about having the AudioFile and the eight simultaneous tracks you can cut with is that you're able not only to manipulate sound but to hear all the things in sync with one another, so the incoming whizzes relate directly to the explosion, the bullet whizzes relate directly to the gunshot, and so on, and you can lay them out in groups before you mix.

"A group of us worked for a month from 7 p.m. to 4 a.m. doing effects redubbing. It was hard work, but obviously it was worth it. I'm very happy with how it all came out."

Alan Howarth: Story of a Leg Man

A top independent sound designer, Alan Howarth has worked on such special effects extravaganzas as *Back to the Future III*, *Die Hard II*, *Total Recall*, *Firebirds* and *RoboCop 2*. His Electric Melody Studio, which recently moved to Santa Monica, is equipped with a 60-channel Neve V3 console, a variety of different recorders and the requisite outboard gear to be competitive. We chatted about the work he did on *RoboCop 2*, a film that seems to have used just about every effects person in Hollywood at one time or another.

"I got involved with *RoboCop 2* in the second go-around, actually," Howarth says. "There was a whole design that went into the big Kane monster [RoboCop's arch enemy in the film] that Steven Flick, the sound designer/editor, did. He thought he had it covered, but when he played it for the director, he didn't like it. So the robot was split up into different parts for different people to work on, because time was getting short. I handled the lower torso and the leg servos; Joel Valentine of Todd AO/Glen Glenn did the upper torso; John P., one of the original guys on it, had the arms; and they kept the footsteps from the original. It sounds like that could be problematic, but actually it worked out well. Because each guy took his own approach, there was a lot of variety to the sounds. If I or someone else had done the whole robot, it might have turned out more homogenous. Mine was like ultra-realistic servos and clinking; Joel's was more sci-fi comedic, with synth sweeteners and things like that; and John P. had a combination of servos and synth sweeteners.

"I worked up ten different versions of the leg and showed them to Steve Flick. The one we went with was a DAT recording of the servo on a 1968

LTD convertible top. I used Sennheiser 441s on it. It had a nice bass: *guh-eeeeshhh!* So each time the robot would move, you'd hear this great servo sound, and we had big, clunky footsteps to go with it; it was a nice contrast. At the same time, I had some other servos and I only used the end clink—when a servo goes to the end of the travel it sort of buckles up against whatever the mechanism is. So I used that. It was a combination of events that became the movement.

"Then the trick was to come up with about seven different lengths of this movement, because we didn't want them to all sound the same. We wanted different-sized steps and different rates. So I went into the Synclavier and chopped up the effect. Basically, I pulled the center out of the servo travel from the original, which was maybe four seconds long, down to one that was maybe a half-second long. From there, [the effects editors] gave me the cut track of the footsteps transferred to a 1/2-inch 4-track with time code. I got my old LinnDrum, took an audio trigger off the down of the footstep, and got a MIDI hitlist that I put on one track of the Synclavier. I dragged all the hits to the right-sized servo footsteps, and then I split it into left and right footsteps, which you needed for some close-up shots.

"So there was a batch of effects from me for the legs, a batch for the upper torso, more for the arms. Then someone had to sit at a Moviola and make the little one- and two-frame corrections to get it all to work, because it had to be coordinated with everything else—the torso had to move with the legs and so forth. That can drive you crazy. My part alone took about eight days, though I did a few other sounds during that time, too. When they suck RoboCop up with a giant electromagnet—that was mine, too. But that's another story." ✿

> "To record authentic bullet whizzes for *Glory*, Civil War re-enactors shot live rounds at our sound guy. It was very, very effective." —Lon Bender

Digital Post

"**FOR SALE: ONE BOX OF RAZOR BLADES,** formerly used for audio post-production. Employed on impressive list of films. Will sell to highest bidder or will donate to audio museum."

We may not be seeing ads like that any time soon, but the fact is that the current generation of digital audio workstations and disk recorders have made an enormous impact on the way post-production professionals do their jobs. Long nights of splicing miniscule bits of mag tape and fullcoat are virtually over for dialog cutters and effects wizards, who are benefitting from the many advantages of working on disk-based systems. To find out how this first generation of workstations makes the day-to-day grind of post work a little easier, we queried a number of end-users.

John Ross, Digital Sound and Picture, Los Angeles—Doremi Digital Audio Workstation Nucleus

We have five DAWN systems and we've been very happy with them. The DAWN is basically an 8-track, disk-based recording system that works with the Macintosh at the front end, and it's set up in an interactive fashion—you can get in and move snippets of audio around. It's very flexible, and its use of the Mac allowed us to get into networking. We've set up an Ethernet system linking all five of our 8-track systems together, allowing us to do file transfers and sound pooling and things of that nature. We can also use any Macintosh peripherals for archiving, such as magneto-optical or whatever we may want to use later.

We use [Digidesign] Sound Tools systems here—we have three of them with SampleCell setups, and they also hang on the network. The DAWN has the ability to work with AIFF files, as does Sound Tools/SampleCell, so we can basically swap files between the dialog editors and the effects editors on the network. It makes for a very powerful system, and allows a number of people to work at the same time: all the advantages of a mainframe-style system.

We do a lot of Fox movies here, such as *Seeds of Tragedy*. In a case like that, when a tape comes in, a dialog editor working on a DAWN will split the dialog out into its various components: typically into eight tracks, which include the dialog and production effects and all. We build and balance with fade ins and fade outs across the eight tracks of a DAWN unit. This information is then integrated with the ADR, and various fills and takes are created to make it work in different interpretations, depending on how the director wants to hear it. It's all pre-built on the hard disk. When we mix, the dialog elements come from another DAWN, which is in the mixing stage. The background sound effects—birds, traffic and various long continuing sound effects—are also cut on the DAWN system and split across eight tracks. Then all the hard effects are built in the SampleCell system, and we do Foley on the multitrack. So at the end of the day, you're mixing Foleys from

Sound Designers And Editors Talk About the New G-G-Generation Of DAWs

BY BLAIR JACKSON

the multitrack, dialog from one DAWN, background elements on another DAWN and hard effects from a SampleCell system.

Alan Howarth, Electric Melody Studios, Santa Monica— NED Synclavier

I've been using the Synclavier [9600] for a long time. We have 40 MB of RAM in the 9600 we have now, and that's good for stereo backgrounds up to about 90 seconds and still have two backgrounds up, so you can A-B cut. We hope to do all our background cutting to the PostPro in the future.

With any of these systems, the library that goes with it is critical. You can run out and buy the latest whiz-bang, high-technology, magneto-optical, everything's-in-there machine, but you can't turn around and do a job with it until you take some time to get some stuff into the machine, and get a backlog to the point where it's sort of off-the-shelf. I've had the Synclavier for several years and we're on our 16th optical, which gives us about 32 gigabytes of effects—this is getting serious! This is the kind of density it takes to have somebody walk in here and give them a show in a relatively short period of time.

An interesting show we did in conjunction with LucasArts is a film called *Salmonberries*, directed by Percy Aldon, who made *Baghdad Cafe*. It stars [country singer] k.d. lang as an Eskimo woman who's trying to find her identity. There was almost no music in this show; instead it was all sound effects, but the director didn't want layers and layers of effects. It became an example of minimalist sound design, where we really had to give the director the right thing for each scene. The big elements were wind and dogs—dogs because in these Alaskan towns there might be 4,000 people and 15,000 dogs, so orchestrating these dog sounds became one of our big tasks.

[Aldon] had recorded some production dogs during the filming, and then we collected as many other dogs—and some wolves, too—as we could. I took the production recordings, put them in the Synclavier, spliced out all the unwanted material to get to the essence of dog howls, and sequenced the dog stuff, really orchestrating the sounds to the action. We did a lot of envelope shaping on the dogs to get the right moments to synchronize through all these dog choruses. There were several scenes, too, that really let me stretch out on the Synclavier and do some multichannel sound design. Because I've got the multiple outputs I was able to use individual sequencer tracks, quadruple them, assign four outputs to four different sequencer tracks. Then I went through with the mod wheel, doing some delays and creating quad panning among the four sequencer tracks, firing them out at real time.

"With any of these systems, the library that goes with it is critical. You can run out and buy the latest whiz-bang, high-technology, magneto-optical, everything's-in-there machine, but you can't turn around and do a job with it until you have some stuff in the machine."
—Alan Howarth

The Opus Room at Blue
Light Sound

Jeff Largent, Blue Light Sound, Burbank—Lexicon Opus

We worked on the Jean-Claude Van Damme martial arts flick *Double Impact*, and it had lots of footsteps, lots of bangs, lots of props, lots of effects. I concentrated on the Foley, and actually Foley is the main reason Blue Light got an Opus. The owner, Bob Rutledge, wanted to get something that would give us really clean Foley. So far, we haven't been doing a lot of editing within Opus, simply because it's been more profitable to keep the stage where the Opus room is online as long as we can during the day. So we crank the stuff out, dump it out from Opus eight tracks at a time to single-stripe and usually let the film editors cut it.

Actually, though, there was a project we edited within Opus—a film about a female serial killer. It was very interesting; it was a completely different approach to doing a traditional Foley session. Instead of just saying, "Yeah, that's going to cover it," or backing up and punching in, I have the ability to not only do all of that, but also to very rapidly bring editing into the picture by doing a quick edit—position things, pull tracks up, splice some air into it, all the things to make sure the footsteps are going to be where we want them.

In that film we did eight tracks of footsteps, movement, props. We were working with a very limited budget so we kept it all in an 8-track environment. We would build as many as 16 or 17 tracks and then edit and consolidate down to an 8-track playback, spit the whole thing out to Dolby SR 2-inch, and then they'd mix from that.

The great thing about Opus is its 99 tracks, so I bring up the first set of eight—maybe it's eight tracks of props. I sub them to two tracks on the SR, put the original source tracks away, call up eight more tracks of footsteps. I play back the submix, and add more footstep submix to it. As I add it, I realize that, say, one prop needs to come down, so I recall the mix that has that prop on it, fix it, punch it in, and we're done. For a desk that's only 12 modules and eight disk events back at any given time, the 99 tracks really come into play because you can build wider and wider than the desk can do at any given moment, sub down and pull it back.

Rick Schwartz, Music Animals, Los Angeles—Studer Dyaxis

We did some spots for Nike that really turned out well, and they were done almost entirely within the Dyaxis. One of them, a spot with [tennis star] Andre Agassi, was unique because Nike wanted it to be sound design only—no voice-overs, no music—just sound. So it really gave us the opportunity to go crazy. We started out with some stuff that had been recorded in the field. It sounded way too wimpy, so we ended up re-recording just about everything.

We brought in tennis rackets and we did our own swishes, ball hits and everything else. We basically recorded all our own sounds into the Dyaxis. We learned that the best swishes came from hitting with the racket sideways. All the ball hits were pitched down using Passport Alchemy software and extensively digitally EQ'd to make them sound the way we wanted. We probably had 300 sound effects in that 30-second commercial, and they were all built in Dyaxis. We used bottle rockets for some of the swishes; we used pile drivers for ball hits; we used backward cannon for his pre-serve wind-up. Lot of pitching up and down, a lot of level changes, enveloping. Reality never plays; you've got to go bigger. And I think it works.

Rick Schwartz

One of the things we find useful about Dyaxis is that it doesn't have any arbitrary limits. The system we were using has two outputs, but there are unlimited internal tracks. Basically the spot was recorded, mixed and EQ'd entirely in the Dyaxis.

After we approved the mix, the tracks were transferred back into Dyaxis. They said the ending was a little too wet, so we slugged in a couple of changes and saved a whole remix.

Harry Snodgrass, Vision Trax/20th Century Fox, Los Angeles—Digidesign Sound Tools

For a film I did a while ago, *Predator 2*, we used Sound Tools to create the voice of the creature—loading in a lot of animals, human voices, different kinds of machinery—playing with the pitch and reversing sounds. We used it in odd ways, too: using the scrubbing feature but taking that scrubbed sound and actually transferring that off again while I was scrubbing. Also, we integrated the whole thing into a different environment, not just staying with the Mac—in other words, dumping things off in real time and then dumping them back in and working with them. We also used it to pre-layer a lot of those sounds to create the voice of the creature, making it as big and monstrous as we could.

It seems as though we often work with directors who like to change their films up until the very last minute. Actually, even beyond that—we've changed films *after* they've been optically printed. We work on a lot of those big extravaganzas where it's a full-effects show. And if you go to multitrack you're screwed because we sometimes get two sets of changes a day, with 20 picture changes, and we'll have hundreds of units to change. We might have one whole crew that's just doing changes. And Sound Tools is great for that.

I use it in more subtle ways, too. I did a film for Fox called *29th Street*, which is more of a talky film, and for that I used Sound Tools to create and layer backgrounds before they got to the stage—it's less complicated. In other words, I did things like making a ghetto background with different people and different areas and doing a layer of that, so we didn't walk into the stage with 25 tracks just to create one background.

Lew Goldstein, EFX Systems, Burbank—NED PostPro

EFX totally revolves around the Synclavier and the Direct-to-Disk [PostPro]. We have five Synclavs and two PostPros, and complementing those we have eight Sony PCM-3324 digital multitracks, so we're a large digital house.

The hardest part about the digital domain is dialog editing, partially be-

"We did a Nike spot with [tennis star] Andre Agassi that Nike wanted to be sound design only—no voiceovers, no music. We used bottle rockets for some of the swishes; we used pile drivers for ball hits; we used backward cannon for the preserve wind-up. Reality never plays; you've got to go bigger."
—Rick Schwartz

cause dialog editors using tape and mag have incorporated some idiosyncratic techniques. They use amazing tricks to make production dialog work. It's a weird animal because you have directors talking, you have different pieces coming from different takes with varied inflections, and editors have come up with odd ways to fix those problems. So to take a very logical machine and try to do the same thing is difficult, to say the least. And I think a lot of companies haven't had a good idea of how dialog editors actually work.

Recently we've been getting into using the edit decision list conform on the PostPro. To my knowledge, the machine that does the conforming the best is the PostPro. It is capable of taking your production dialog from whatever format it was originally cut from—say 1-inch if it was a TV-type conform, or 1/4-inch with time code, or even DAT with time code—and record it to the edit points, plus recording 3- or 4-second handles on either side of the edit point. I can go in on the edit view or the sequence editor and grab the in-time of the edited cue, open it and have that three or four seconds of audio before the cue that might have fills or other pieces of dialog that I might want to cheat in and use. So once the material is conformed, a lot of the extra source material I'll need is already loaded with it.

The edit view is a convenient way of editing: To see a graphic representation of your block and to see a cue of audio with a ramp at the front and back is a great feature. Some editors would probably rather see waveforms—which you can do with the PostPro, though it's more complicated—but as an editor I've always relied more on hearing what I'm cutting than *seeing* what I'm cutting. I can scrub across all of my eight tracks, hearing them simultaneously, and all of the audio under the playhead of the machine. So I have quick access to any aspect of the sound audibly. And it's probably one of the best scrub sounds of any of the machines.

I did dialog cutting on a relatively low-budget film called *Neon City*. The mag tracks were put into the machine, and I then spent about two or three days with another editor rolling through and splitting all the mags out to their individual edits. That's unbelievably simple on the PostPro. You just roll through, make a point, make another point, and split that piece out. Once I had my basic split I went back in, found the pieces that I'd split out that were either clipped from the mag edit or just poor quality, and slowly replaced each of those pieces. Once I had that, I ran down each reel and did my fills, fades, and crossing in and out of the different tracks. For a low-budget situation where we didn't have the money for a total rebuild, it worked out quite well.

Hans Zimmer and Jay Rifkin, Media Ventures, Los Angeles— Akai DD1000 Disk Recorder

Zimmer: We used the DD1000 on *Thelma & Louise*. The ending kept changing; originally there weren't going to be any opening titles. Then after it was basically done, Ridley [Scott, the film's director] suddenly decided he wanted some titles after all. We recorded most of the music for it in London with English musicians. Once I was back here I wasn't able to get the original musicians, and we didn't really have time for that anyway. So we just started hacking things up in the DD1000 and making up new cues completely out of old bits—take the drums from one piece and something else from another. The DD1000 is great for sticking things together and trying things out without investing too much time in the process. The challenge for all of us is to stop thinking about these various machines as just tape machines without razor blades, because you can do much more interesting things with them.

Rifkin: Aside from taking different instruments from different cues on *Thelma & Louise* and assembling them all, we supplemented that with new recordings as well—I can't remember now if it was MIDI-triggered or SMPTE-triggered. So we were using the DD1000 as a tape recorder, but because of instant access, it made it possible to write over it using sequencers and so forth. To continue, or adapt or loop different pieces was very quick, and I think it's safe to say we couldn't have done what we did without it.

One of the things I like is that in some ways you can look on it as a musical instrument. It can be MIDI-driven, so if your sequencer is SMPTE-driven it's easier to have the DD1000 MIDI-driven. Then when tape isn't running, you're still listening to it, so it's actually slaved to your sequencer in that kind of application most of the time. It's easier going into the sequencer and offsetting it in whatever direction you want, manipulating it there, than going into the DD1000 and going into a cue list and nudging it back and forth. But it's a good combination in that way.

The other thing I'd say is that I don't know of anything that does as long a crossfade. You can do up to 60 seconds, and it accepts and puts out every digital format I know about: optical, SCSI, its own DBus, as well as handling sample rate conversion.◉

Terminator 2: Judgment Day

Behind The Scenes with The *T2* Sound Team

BY TOM KENNY

THE CAMERA PANS ACROSS burned-out car bodies, charred carousel horses, a bent and fragile teeter-totter—a broken playground from the year 2029 A.D. A desolate wind is all you hear. Then CRUNCH! A robotic foot crushes a vacant human skull. Lasers, explosions, screams. Here comes *Terminator 2: Judgment Day*.

What hasn't been written about *T2*? A hundred million dollars to make, some claim, though it actually brought in more than $200 million in domestic sales alone. It came together in just a shade over a year, from first rough draft to its July 3, 1991, release date. Would it surprise anyone at this point that the sound of the wind in the opening scene comes from the crack of an open door to the main mix room at Skywalker Sound, and the sound of the crushed skull is actually a pistachio being crunched by a metal plate?

The re-recording on *T2* began at Skywalker Sound, San Rafael, Calif., on May 23, and it ended on June 21. That's four weeks, from premix to final to 70mm CDS master. And this is a big movie. With big sound.

"We had every mix room in the facility going," says Gloria Borders, sound supervisor. "We re-recorded all the effects in the movie before the crew came on—all the motorcycles, guns, cars, semis—knowing that when the crew came on we were going to have four weeks to cut the thing, and it *had* to be ready to go."

Two weeks before the premix, the film was still 2 hours and 45 minutes long. Because of a clause in writer/director/producer James Cameron's contract, a week before the premix it was cut to 2 hours 15 minutes. "We had about 2,000 units built, ready to mix," Borders says, "and they cut 30 minutes. It meant going into every single unit to take out a foot, then another bit, then 30 feet, then 50 feet. A lot of patchwork was done. We had 35 editors and assistants, and we worked non-stop. After we premixed it, we had very few picture changes, which was wonderful because then we could just go into the final, and that was where Gary Rydstrom took over and did a genius of a job."

Rydstrom, sound designer and re-recording mixer, would be the first to admit that he had plenty of help. Beside him at the SSL 5000 for the final sat Gary Summers for the music mix and Tom Johnson on dialog. All three credit the editors for delivering quality units under pressure. And through it all stood James Cameron, a hands-on director till the end.

"[Cameron's] approach to sound is hyper-realistic," Rydstrom says. "I

wouldn't call it stylized, but everything is very big, and you can make it movie-sized. But he also likes it to be fairly authentic—realistic, but hyper-realistic. A testosterone approach to match what he's doing with the visuals.

"Your first thought when you see a lot of special effects is that sound's job is to not only do something as fantastical as the visual, but also to make it real. It's not competing with the special visual effect, because people perceive the visual and the sound differently. [Sound designer] Walter Murch had a way of putting it: 'The eyes are the front door, and the ears are the back door.'"

SOUND EFFECTS

The gathering of sound elements began unofficially in November 1990, when Rydstrom visited the steel mill set used for the climactic final sequence in the film. Production granted post-production two days of access to the mill, and two Skywalker recordists, armed with Sony 2000

R-DATs, came back with seven hours of metal and machines on tape.

"Most of what's in the film is ambience, like steam hisses, metal clanging, conveyor belts," Rydstrom explains. "The conveyor belt that Arnold comes up on in the end before shooting T-1000 is a conveyor belt from the steel mill. In the fight scene [between the two Terminators] you hear some of the sheet metal being dropped."

From November on, sounds were gathered, often from the field, and sometimes created in the studio. Video arcades, car crusher junkyards, and all the vehicles and guns were recorded to DAT. The sound for the motorcycle that Arnold drives comes from a Harley owned by a construction worker at Skywalker Ranch. People brought in dirt bikes, SWAT vans and all sorts of specific vehicles. Though production provided the actual motorcycles and semis from the film, they were used mainly for suspension squeaks and running over boards, not for engine sounds.

Production also provided many of the guns used in the film, including the hard-to-find Mini Gun that Arnold uses in the police shootout outside the Cyberdyne building. Three recordists went to the Stembridge shooting range outside of L.A., two with R-DATs and one with a Nagra (with Dolby A card). "I was thinking of combining the R-DAT version with the Nagra," Rydstrom says, "trying to get the snap of the digital sound. It usually has a nice transient snap to it but sometimes doesn't have the full-body punch of the Nagra." The R-DATs were coupled with Sanken M-S mics; the Nagra had a Neumann on one channel, Schoeps on the other.

When you record a Mini Gun at full speed, Rydstrom says, it doesn't sound like a machine gun but a cannon. So, it was recorded at less than top speed, then speeded up in the mix, with a touch of EQ added and a thunderclap from the house library to sweeten the initial burst of sound.

"That was a fun scene to do," Rydstrom says. "The difficulty was that he is so in control of shooting this gun that the destruction he creates has to be within reason. It has to be such that you don't believe a lot of cops are dying. So, we couldn't use ricochets, because standard Hollywood ricochets would imply that the bullets were flying out of control and killing somebody. And we couldn't use explosions on the cars, which look like they are exploding, because they weren't exploding. They were just being demolished to the point where they would collapse. It was tricky to just use hits on metal and glass breaks and suspension drops and ricochets that sounded like thuds."

The wind sounds, so ominous in the beginning of the film and so prominent in the desert scene, were often performed off of a Synclavier. "Some of that, I have to admit, is me going 'whooooo,'" Rydstrom notes. "Some of it is from the door to the mix room that I usually work in. By playing it on the Synclavier, you can put in as long a loop as you can afford to. You set the octave ratio on the keyboard so that it's not in usual steps—much smaller musical steps—then you just put long attacks and decays on the wind and ride the pitch wheel. Very often you can perform the wind while watching the picture."

The biggest sound design challenge, however, was the sound of the T-1000 Terminator moving into and out of liquid metal, the quality that makes him virtually indestructible. "It's not really liquid, because it doesn't look like mud," Rydstrom says. "It doesn't have any bubbles in it. It doesn't gurgle. It doesn't do anything visually except flow like mercury. But mercury doesn't make a sound. It's very silent."

So Rydstrom and Tom Myers, his assistant, developed a number of sound elements, sampled them into a Synclavier and played them against picture to see what worked. When the T-1000 is flowing and transforming, that's Rydstrom spraying Dust-Off into a flour and water mixture, with a condom-sealed mic stuck in the goo. "It would make these huge goopy bubbles," he says. "And the moment when the bubble is forming, it has this sound that's similar to a cappucino maker or a milk steamer. Funny enough, it had this metallic quality to it, so I believed it. And it also had an evolving quality to it, so I believed it for transformation."

For the sound of bullets hitting T-1000, Rydstrom slammed an inverted glass into a bucket of yogurt, getting a hard edge to accompany the goop. The sound of T-1000 passing through steel bars is nothing more than dog food being slowly sucked out of a can. "A lot of that I would play backward or do something to," Rydstrom explains, "but those were the basic elements. What's amazing to me is the combination of Industrial Light & Magic using millions of dollars of high-tech digital equipment to come up with the visuals, and meanwhile I'm inverting a dog food can."

> For the sound of bullets hitting T-1000, Rydstrom slammed an inverted glass into a bucket of yogurt, getting a hard edge to accompany the goop. The sound of T-1000 passing through steel bars is nothing more than dog food being slowly sucked out of a can.

MUSIC

"I think the score in this movie works as the driving element that holds parts of the mix together," Rydstrom says, "something that keeps driving the scene forward without telegraphing the suspense. Using score in that way has been done so much that it loses its impact. So we did other things to give dynamics to the scene. It's not traditional screeching violins leading up to a fight scene." Often it is just a soft "boom boom" from the percussion track, as when Arnold lands his Harley after a short, silent flight in the canal chase scene. And sometimes it's delicate guitar in the desert.

The soft yet militaristic score was composed by Brad Fiedel and mixed in the final by Gary Summers. Fiedel was on the tightest of tight schedules, still composing as the mix was taking place, sometimes delivering cues for the second half of a reel as the first was being finished. It wouldn't have been possible, according to Summers, without Fiedel's chain of three Fairlights.

"He did all the sampling and sequencing from the Fairlights," Summers says. "He would do that over to 24-track and mix down. Then he would deliver to me, per cue, two or three 3-tracks—basically a left-center-right mix of percussion, strings and maybe some synths. He would separate out the different groups so that we could rebalance or whatever.

"[The score] was mixed very well by Brad," Summers adds. "I did very little to it, some EQ and reverb occasionally. I had a 224 and two Quantecs for the music, so I could filter it in as well as put it into rooms. I like the rooms on the Quantec—the small-room programs are great."

T2 was mixed in a THX monitoring environment, and no surround sound was laid on the masters. "Surround is what we call magic surround," Summers says. "The out-of-phase component will automatically go to surround. Now when I'm making the 70mm master, we have our 18 channels into the board—music, dialog and effects separate. I take the left-center-right of the music and I send that to left-center-right of the 70mm master. But I also feed it into the DS4, and I bring that up in the console and add it in as a discrete surround.

"We were mixing in a discrete, split-surround 70mm format," he continues, "and in the monitor mix I was listening to that magic surround component. I was hearing the whole time what was going to happen, although none of it was going down on tape. It's a little bit complicated, but it worked out real well, and it gave me free tracks on the recorder."

DIALOG AND FOLEY

According to Gloria Borders, around 70% of the dialog in the film and most of the breathing is ADR, which shouldn't surprise anyone since most of the movie takes place on the run. By all accounts, the looping performances were excellent, even those by Eddie Furlong (playing the 10-year-old John Connor), whose voice grew deeper during the nine months of production.

"I actually had to pitch all of his loops up quite a bit," says dialog mixer Tom Johnson. "I ended up using the Lexicon 2400—a device used mainly by TV studios—which will actually speed up or slow down a tape machine, or whatever, and pitch it accordingly so you don't get a pitch change. Using the AMS or even the Lexicon 480 pitch programs, you get artifacts after one percent or so. I was having to pitch the kid between three percent and four percent."

ADR constantly had to be matched to production dialog within scenes, sometimes within sentences. In the hospital scene where Linda Hamilton watches herself revealing her nuclear holocaust dreams on a TV monitor, the first half is from production, on 1/4-inch and videotape, the second half ADR. Johnson matched them up, then futzed it in the final mix. "All I had to do was match the natural room echo, which is easy if you get lucky. I used a Lexicon 480.

"I feel that it's important to retain as much of the natural sound of the production dialog as possible, smoothing the backgrounds out by using handles, or whatever," Johnson adds. "The editors give me handles on both sides of the line, and I just have to do a bunch of crossfades to make it sound like it was recorded by a microphone in one take. Then I smooth it out as much as possible, taking out weird tones with notch filters or really sharp parametric EQs.

"Rather than using noise gates, I'll clean the track up as much as possible with EQ," Johnson continues. "There is a device that Dolby makes, and I think they're finally building more of them, called the 430. It uses a Dolby SR card and some other stuff to create a sort of sophisticated noise gate. It allows you to clean backgrounds up, but it doesn't sound like a noise gate where it's pumping a lot."

Johnson also helped premix two reels of Foley, and it was the Foley team that had perhaps the least time.

Since it would have been a nightmare to conform all the Foley elements to picture changes during the week before the premix, it was decided to hold off on Foley recording. "We decided to gamble and record Foley as close to the final as possible," says Gloria Borders. "We learned to take that chance on *Godfather III*. The final mix for *T2* started on June 6, and I think we were done with the last reel of Foley on June 10."

Despite the rush, it is flawless Foley, performed by Dennie Thorpe and recorded by Christopher Boyes. "Most audiences have no idea that we replaced all the leather creaks on the Terminator's jacket," Rydstrom says, "and the buckle clinks, and the footsteps—all the incidental movements have been replaced.

"I think the shining moment for Foley in this movie is when Sarah is getting out of her straps in her hospital bed," Rydstrom continues. "She takes the paper clip, spits it out, it lands on the bed, she puts it in the buckle, she gets out of her strap, and she uses the paper clip to pick the lock of the door. The whole scene is nothing but Foley and music. And a lot of the tension is coming from focusing in on those little sounds from Foley—the paper clip into the tumblers of the lock."

Long after you leave *Terminator 2*, it's the small sounds, and the silences, that you remember more than the explosions. When Arnold shoots the frozen T-1000 in the steel mill, all background ambience fades out in the split second before the gun goes off. And when Arnold flies on the Harley, the engine, the music, everything cuts out until he lands.

"I learned on this film that silence works even for an extended period of time," Rydstrom says. "The biggest mixing challenge was making everything be loud, at least apparently loud, when a lot of the time you have loud things happening simultaneously and in a row. It's not always easy to make something huge. I love moments like when the Cyberdyne building blows up—when the big explosion of the building is preceded just by a long period of silence and the click of a detonator." ◔

Malcolm X

M ALCOLM X IS OUT! And *Malcolm X* is big! Step back from the controversy for a minute. Forget about Amiri Baraka and the various claims on who can best represent Malcolm X to the world. Forget about flag burning and rights to the Rodney King video. Forget about corporate budgets and the call to skip work and school. Look at this film. *Listen* to this film.

Spike Lee has pieced together a one-of-a-kind project, certainly his most ambitious to date. The storyline, written by Arnold Perl and Spike Lee and adapted from *The Autobiography of Malcolm X* as told to Alex Haley, predates Malcolm's birth and continues after his death. Location shoots ranged from the streets of Harlem to the Egyptian desert to the slums of Soweto to the holy city of Mecca (the first Western film crew allowed in, we are told). And it's beautifully shot by cinematographer Ernest Dickerson and edited by Barry Brown, with that bold visual style we've come to associate with Spike.

"It's not a totally personal film," Spike says while watching over the final mix, "because Malcolm X was somebody who lived and breathed. But I think that was the challenge, to make it a personal film and at the same time respect that it is somebody's life. I can't just do anything I want with it. Still, anybody who has seen my work and looks at this film will be able to tell that I did it."

By the same token, anybody who has *listened* to Spike's work will notice similarities in *Malcolm X*. The core sound team has been together since *Do the Right Thing* (1989), through *Mo' Better Blues* (1990) and *Jungle Fever* (1991): re-recording mixer Tom Fleischman, supervising sound editor Skip Lievsay and music supervisor Alex Steyermark. (Lievsay and Fleischman also work together for a number of other East Coast directors, among them Scorsese, Demme and Sayles.) The final mix took place over 13 weeks in Studio D of Sound One, New York City. Fleischman, mixing only his second discrete 6-track film, sat solo behind the 60-input Neve with Necam 96 automation.

This is New York, and unlike L.A. where three people sit down for the final, a single re-recording mixer is the norm. Fleischman, who looks considerably younger than his 41 years, moves like a large cat up and down the board, intensely focused on the screen. Behind him or beside him sit Skip, Spike and Alex, with various ears walking in and out of the room. Phones ring silently and constantly. There are no decisions by committee—Spike definitely has final say on whether a particular sound stays or goes or is altered—though there is considerable decision-making by consensus.

X didn't involve any particular revolutions in soundtrack creation, though the process was complex in its subtlety. By all accounts, the biggest difficulties had to do with the sheer size and scope of the project. The film is three hours and thirty-one minutes long and it's chock full of dialog, music and Foley, which means a helluva lot of material to sort through. As more than

The Lush Sound Of Spike Lee's Biggest Film

BY TOM KENNY

Denzel Washington as
Malcolm X at Harlem's
Apollo Theater

one person commented, it was like working on two movies.

The film is 20 reels long, but the mixing process remains the same: Start with the dialog predub and mix it down to two 6-tracks, one being production dialog and ADR, the other being group ADR. That takes four weeks, which Fleischman admits is a luxurious schedule. Then start on effects, mixed down to three 6-tracks, while monitoring the dialog. Play those back against Foley, which is mixed down to another two 6-tracks, and when the three predubs are finished, bring in music for the final. On average, Fleischman can get through a double reel a day (about 20 minutes of film) once the predubs are finished. For *Malcolm X*, a double-reel takes a day-and-a-half. The final print master eventually goes out on a single 6-track, mixed down from three 6-track full-coat stems. If you have the opportunity, see the SR•D (Dolby 6-track digital) print; it's also being released in 70mm and 35mm with Dolby SR.

"This is the third time we've done 70 mm but the first time we've done a discrete mix," says Lievsay. "We went out of our way to have as much as possible in the 6-track format. The music, sound effects and voice-over were recorded in 6-track, 4-track, quad and stereo, to achieve something special-sounding. We didn't break any new ground, but I think taken together they make for a very lush soundtrack."

Lush is the perfect word to describe the soundtrack and the picture. Too often we associate "good" sound with explosive, attention-grabbing effects, when the reality is that the best tracks are usually the ones we don't notice. *X* certainly has big sound, and Spike likes it loud, but in no way is the sound distracting. Creative? Yes. Up front? Certainly. But you will remember Denzel Washington's (who plays Malcolm X) oratory long after you've forgotten the sound of the Molotov cocktail crashing through Malcolm's window.

Dialog, ADR and Voice-Over

"Dialog is king," Fleischman says. "If you don't hear the dialog, you don't get the story. The hardest scenes to mix are never the big action scenes—those kind always mix themselves. You just open up what you have and it's a matter of balance. The most difficult, tedious work

Spike Lee on location at
The Apollo

in any film is a small, intimate scene between two people, particularly if there is no music.

"For example, there's a scene between Malcolm and his wife talking in a room, just the two of them," he continues. "Then the camera pans across the room and there's some dolly motor noise in the track, along with some clothing rustles. When the dialog editors prepared it, they removed as much of the dolly noise as they could and replaced it with clean room tone. The problem was that where those sections were lifted out and replaced, the clothing rustle suddenly popped up. So every time there was a splice, you could hear the clothing pop. Nothing was covering it satisfactorily, and we got to the final before we solved it by adding a little bit of rain."

If that represents the puzzle-solving tedium of film mixing, then the "fun" must come in scenes where there are rapid cuts from live-action, wide-screen 35mm to a grainy, black-and-white, 16mm image. Usually the switch takes place when the press is surrounding Malcolm, offering the illusion of a documentary perspective circa 1965.

Dialog tracks came in on 1/4-inch, were transferred to 35mm mag, then cut on Moviolas by Kevin Lee, Magdaline Volaitis and Philip Stockton at C5 Inc., Lievsay's home-base editorial house that he owns with three partners. ADR (and there was a lot of it) was supervised by Gail Showalter and recorded mainly in Sound One's Studio K by Dave Boulton: six hundred main character lines; small lines; crowd sessions at BMG; and voice-over. Roughly 25 percent of the film dialog was ADR, according to Lievsay.

"The actors were extremely good loopers," Lievsay says. "I boomed a lot of the looping myself, and we tried to guess where the boom mic was in the sync recording, the idea being to place the ADR microphones in a similar position to match the production track better. And it does. That's a pretty good technique that we're starting to use more and more. Also, that way I have something to do besides sit in the session and say, 'Faster, slower. Non-sync, in-sync.'"

Voice-over tends to work best in film when it somehow stands apart from the action and does not act as a storytelling device. The voice-over in *Malcolm X*, Denzel Washington reading passages from *The Autobiography of Malcolm X* over picture, works for precisely that reason. It also works because it sounds different. It sounds rich and full. It has presence.

Lievsay came up with the idea of recording the voice-over in multimic stereo in the big room at BMG Studios. Washington spoke from a podium with a Neumann U87 out front, a lavalier on his lapel, and a pair of Schoeps cardioids left and right. When the omnidirectional Neumann picked up too much of the room, it was filtered down and backfilled with the lavalier, which also brought a sort of "chesty resonance" to the tracks, a "mechanical proximity," Lievsay says.

"By doing it multimic, we can take advantage of the three speakers up front [in the theater] instead of just one," he adds. "The voice-over can then be separated and be perceived [by the audience] to be different. Also, you can make it much louder. You can have voice-over over dialog and maintain the separation. You can have voice-over, music and effects all playing together at a louder volume. You can play with perspectives, like music playing out one side and effects the other. It basically multiplies the number of options by three."

"We wanted to make sure that there was a dramatic quality difference between the voice-over and the sync dialog," Fleischman adds, offering a mixer's view. "You try to find a balance between the two center mics—the 87 and the lavalier—then balance that with whatever you're using from the left-right Schoeps pair. We then treated it with the SPL Vitalizer, a psychoacoustic equalizer. It synthesizes upper and lower harmonics, sort of like a [dbx 120] boom box except that it also works on the high end. It brings a lot more presence to the upper end of the spectrum and a very deep low end so that the voice sounds full."

Effects and Foley

X is about dialog and words; it is not a big showcase for sound effects. Authentic backgrounds were constructed in stereo, using period cars (from recordings done for the Coen Brothers' *Miller's Crossing*) and non-distinct traffic sounds, accompanied by authentic sirens when necessary. Some motorcycle sounds in the JFK sequence came from work done on *Cool World*. All effects were culled from DAT and CD libraries at C5, then applied creatively.

> "The music, sound effects and voice-overs are very special-sounding and unusual. We didn't break any new ground, but I think taken together they make for a very lush soundtrack." —Skip Lievsay

Anybody can make a building blow up, but not everybody can construct a sinister telephone ring or an increasingly menacing flash bulb sound. Lievsay, who won a Golden Reel for sound effects editing on the Coen Brothers' *Barton Fink*, likes to put elements up there for the mix. If the director doesn't like an effect, it's gone, just as Spike vetoed a gunshot sound that accompanied a telephone slam in Reel 18. Creative use of sound involves risk, and it involves hearing things that sometimes aren't seen on the screen. If it works in the final, great. If it doesn't, move on. The flash bulb sound, cliche as it seems, works.

"There were a lot of elements that Spike encouraged us to tie together with the flash bulb sound," Lievsay says. "There's the idea that fame can be a bad thing politically. Cinematically, the flash bulb has been used for dramatic impact, and that goes through many different films, like *Raging Bull* with its famous flash sounds used as a cinematic device more than a political statement. With *Malcolm X* it is used throughout the film to mark the passage of time and the evolution of Malcolm's character."

Simply put, in the beginning of the film the flashes are innocent; by the end they become distant gunshots. Fleischman calls it a "flash motif." Other threads of association are more subtle. A tiny bullet-by from the JFK motorcade sequence, mixed from left-front to right-rear, reappears later in the film accompanying a swish-pan camera move at one of Malcolm's final press conferences.

Most of the Foley—thousands of cues—was recorded at C5 directly into one of three NED PostPros. "This way we can record and edit without having to do all the transfers," Lievsay explains. "The labor becomes more intensely associated with editing and very little else. Once it's edited, we can transfer to mag—4-track with SR—to bring to the mixing stage. The recording process is pretty streamlined. It's faster; it's suitably cheaper, all things considered; and as a system-wide approach to Foley, it's certainly equal to doing it on film."

As with ADR, Foley is miked from a distance, with EV RE27s handling the metallic sounds, Sanken stereo mics for group effects and Schoeps cardioids for footsteps and the like.

Music

Anybody who has read *The Autobiography* knows that Malcolm loved music, mostly big band jazz. And anybody who's watched Spike Lee's films knows that Spike loves music, all kinds of jazz and everything else. Bring their tastes together, add the emotion of Terence Blanchard's original score, and you have a source soundtrack that's sure to go platinum and a score soundtrack that's sure to gain critical praise. (The source music soundtrack will be released by Quincy Jones' Qwest Records; the score will be released on Spike's new 40 Acres and a Mule Musicworks label.)

> **Anybody can make a building blow up, but not everybody can construct an increasingly menacing flash bulb: In the beginning of *X* the flashes are innocent; by the end they become distant gunshots.**

The score, recorded over three-and-a-half weeks at BMG and ranging from solo piano to intimate jazz trio to 65-piece orchestra, is gorgeous and epic. It's 65 minutes of "Malcolm's Theme," "Betty's Theme," and numerous variations, with Branford Marsalis adding sax overdubs, Blanchard on trumpet and the Harlem Boys Choir lending vocals. Ironically, when the music got bigger, the console got smaller. Overdubs added five more channels, forcing the 60-input Neve into "fader crunch"—not enough inputs. That was solved by a music premix when necessary.

Despite his relatively sophisticated sense of—and use of—score, Spike revels in the use of source music to help tell his story. Score works its way in subtly through the back door to the brain. Source hits you over the head and makes you dance (like Public Enemy's "Fight the Power" from *Do the Right Thing*). It can also make you cry. The *X* credits include Count Basie, Lionel Hampton, Duke Ellington, Ray Charles, Ella Fitzgerald, Billie Holiday, the Ink Spots, Jr. Walker & the All Stars, Aretha Franklin, Sam Cooke, and on and on. Spike picks the music. Spike picks the cues.

"When I hear a song that I really love, I always make a mental note to use it in a film one day. I don't know what film or scene, but eventually I will get it into a movie. This is a perfect example of that, 'A Change Is Gonna Come,'" he says, pointing to the screen. The camera cuts between people converging on the Audubon Ballroom on the day of Malcolm's assassination, February 21, 1965. Sam Cooke's vocals and a beautiful song lead them in. It is perhaps the biggest moment of Spike's biggest film.

Source music comes from various sources, but it's all 2-track masters. The mixer's job is to make each cut sound in line with the rest of the film, to make it as big and wide as the orchestra and as small as the piano or solo trumpet. Because most of the music in the film emanates from a source—i.e., a jukebox, car radio, band onstage—Fleischman first narrowed the image by filtering it and squeezing it down to mono-center. Then reverb was added to fill it up theatrically, both left-right and in the surrounds. Once Foley dance steps, clapping and effects are added, as in the Lionel Hampton "Flying Home" ballroom scene, it's suddenly a full house.

"That recording was made back in the '40s," Fleischman says. "It was originally a mono recording, so we treated it with the Lexicon 480 [and the Vitalizer], using some variations on the set hall programs—one for the left-

Denzel Washington as Malcolm X speaks at a Black Muslim rally.

right, one for the surrounds. That's probably the biggest source cue in the film. The scene was shot to playback with a live orchestra, and if you listen closely you can tell. Spike didn't want to sweeten it at all; he wanted to use the original recording. It's a great piece of music, and I can understand the director not wanting to screw around with it."

One final musical note: Stay for the end credits and you'll hear Aretha Franklin singing "Someday We'll All Be Free." On Friday, September 18, she was in the studio. On Monday afternoon, producer Arif Mardin walked into Sound One with the 4-track masters and a DAT backup under his arm. By Friday, one week later, Aretha was singing over the credit roll, with Blanchard on horn. Who says there's no real drama in a final mix?

Though relatively trouble-free, the final was not without its problems. Some forgotten sounds had to be grabbed, a clock had to be slowed down by removing every other tick, and the effects predub had to be gone through twice. It seems that on Reel 17, Fleischman and Lievsay discovered an effect out of phase. An oscilloscope was brought in, and sure enough, as many as half of the effects were out of phase. Live and learn. Back to Reel 1.

Still, for most of the people who worked on *X*, the relief felt at the end of a long and tiring process will soon be replaced by the realization that they were part of something grand. Spike has said that he was born to direct this picture. Denzel has said he was born to do this part. One person even divided his professional career into Before Malcolm and After Malcolm.

"I learned something about the business," Lievsay says in summation. "I learned that there is a difference between movies like this and other pictures. I probably will never work on another picture quite like this. It was very refreshing, especially in these cynical times.

"You know, I was coming back from Los Angeles and Ossie Davis was on the plane," he continues. "Ossie was a friend of Malcolm X's and he delivered the eulogy at Malcolm's funeral. We have Ossie reading the eulogy in the film. I asked him on the plane if it was the same eulogy, and he said it was. There's something very special about that. It's extremely powerful." ◐

Beauty And The Beast

It Looks And Sounds Like The Classic It Is

BY TOM KENNY

I T IS DIFFICULT TO GET PAST PICTURE and talk about sound for *Beauty and the Beast*. The animation is so rich, detailed and lively that you walk away wondering, "How do they do that? How do they paint a ballroom scene with such spatial textures? How do they so convincingly humanize a candelabra? Who dreamed up those colors?"

Then a little later you start humming the "Belle" song, throwing in an odd lyric or two. The memory of an operatic wardrobe brings a smile. And who can forget the snarls and growls of the wolves on the way to the Beast's castle? The animation, you realize, gives the picture life; the soundtrack gives the picture punch.

The *Beauty and the Beast* project is Walt Disney Pictures' 30th animated feature film, its fifth classic fairy tale adapted for the screen. The project spanned three and a half years and required more than 1 million drawings—226,000 individually painted cels! As is typical in modern Hollywood, the sound engineers for the final mix were allowed four weeks.

Luckily, the re-recording team of Terry Porter, Mel Metcalfe and Dave Hudson—all Buena Vista Sound staffers with impressive sound portfolios—were handed premium elements.

The score included six original songs created by Oscar-winning composer Alan Menken (*The Little Mermaid*), with lyrics by the executive producer, the late Howard Ashman (to whom the film is dedicated). Effects were created by co-supervising sound editors Mark Mangini and Dave Stone of Weddington Productions, with assistance from John Pospisil. And voices? Some of the best from stage and screen: Angela Lansbury, who played Mrs. Potts and sang the title track, David Ogden Stiers, Paige O'Hara, Richard White, Jesse Corti, Rex Everhart, Jo Anne Worley and…Robby Benson as the Beast.

Voicing the Beast

Robby Benson as the Beast? The same boyish voice from *One on One* and *Ice Castles*? Dozens of people auditioned for the part, but Benson sold the producer, directors and everyone else on the strength of his performance, blending the warmth of a human prince with the ferocity of an 8-foot monster. Still, the first question asked of Mangini in his initial interview was "What would you do with the Beast's voice?"

"My suggestion was to re-voice him," Mangini remembers, "a more

Belle and the Beast

stentorian voice that we could grab onto with processing gear to deepen up. But they were sold on the performance, and their biggest concern was 'What can we do to make this better?' I told them quite frankly that I had no clue. I was worried about it. I think I flunked my first interview.

"Actually, I knew then that I would add animal sounds in and around it," Mangini adds. "His performance was just spoken word, but he had to behave like a beast. He was animated to prowl and growl and roar. So we came up with a technique of cutting fore and aft of everything that he said with growls and purrs and things like that from tigers and camels. Then, of course, for sounds that stood in the clear like a big beast roar, it would be stand-alone, processed tiger mixed with camel and bear—live animals, all sounds that I went out and recorded, getting in a pen with my Nagra or DAT.

"Most of the Beast turned out to be camel," Mangini explains. "Camels seemed to be the animal that sounded most like Robby Benson, if that makes any sense. Occasionally, Robby would come into or go out of a line with a growl, trying to make the track as complete as possible. When it was pitched down, some of that sounded okay, and we thought of it as a bridge between Robby's voice and an animal. We figured if we could match his growls with the other material, we would have a seamless blend."

About six months before Mangini started adding in camels, however, lead mixer Terry Porter began experimenting with processing on the voice. According to Porter and others, the timbre just didn't match the visuals, so they brought it into pre-post for a little magic. The main processing tool was a pitch shift program from an Eventide H3000 Ultra-Harmonizer.

"We had to address it line by line and shift him down depending on the delivery," Porter says. "I also found another program on the Eventide that created lower harmonics, which I could add to the voice to reinforce the low end. Besides dropping the voice, this created another part of the voice in the lower spectrum, which helped. I also used a limited-band dbx [120X] boom-box to again reinforce some of the low tones. For a voice, you could get it down way too low, so I had to cut off a lot of low frequencies and pick up a spectrum somewhere between 50 and 100 cycles. That one I used salt-and-pepper—just a little bit."

As expected, once Porter started harmonizing and dropping the voice down, intelligibility became a concern. "We were able to bring back some of the intelligibility with pure equalization on a line-by-line basis," Porter explains, "making sure that we kept a clean top end with a little spike in the upper-mids to put some bite in his voice. When he's angry at the beginning of the movie, I'm using the tools a lot more—much stronger on the low end. And we do decrease that as the movie goes on."

> "A lot of the Beast turned out to be camel. It was the animal that sounded most like Robby Benson." —Mark Mangini

While the Beast's voice was by all accounts the most challenging sound design element, the film lends itself to all sorts of interesting effects and sound moments. The creepy forest that separates the town and castle is filled with plaintive baby cries and cat meows, slowed down to half- or quarter-speed, not to mention the wolf sounds, which are actually 90% pit bulls. The candelabra character, Lumiere, constantly waves his "arms," gesticulating with fire. The fire sound is Foley, because it needed to be articulated to match the action. Foley artist John Rush simply blew across a Sony ECM-50 lavalier mic, and with a little bit of highpassing to take off the rumble, it turned into fire. And just *listen* to the transformation from Beast to prince, the climactic moment when inner beauty reveals itself—it sparkles. Finally, much of the action takes place in a cavernous 18th-century French castle, with all the ambiences that implies.

Reverb, Reverb, Reverb

Back when Mangini and Porter teamed up on *Star Trek IV*, Porter came up with a system for creating a separate reverb premix so that ambience wasn't locked to the dry dialog tracks. That way, if someone didn't like the feel later, it could easily be dumped. But the reverb was textured to fit every scene, so if you needed it, it was there. No futzing in the final.

In this film, Porter and company were dealing with enormous rooms, intimate dinner table settings, courtyards in a storm…you name it. And, of course, the voices and lyrics had to be heard. "I try to mix a dimensional dialog," Porter says. "So often when you're trying to play perspective on dialog, the most common thing is to adjust levels: You want distance, you drop it way back. I find that in the real world—meaning, the audience reaction—dialog gets lost when you drop levels too much for perspective. I try to keep basic levels the same and give dimension with echos, delays and slap echos. I alter levels a little, but not as much as you normally would."

Porter makes extensive use of his Quantec Room Simulator (accessed via the Macintosh) and writes programs into a Lexicon 480. He also uses a Lexicon 200, the Eventide H3000 and even an old 949 for the delays. He often combines, layers and blends into a single machine.

A scene from "Be Our Guest"

"Most of the reverbs that come out of a single machine are really nice," he says. "But in stereo it's good to spread them out left-center-right-surround with multiple reverbs and characteristics, all within one reverb. Normal reverberation in the real world has a lot of different reflection times and distances and contours. On some of the big shots, I would probably have ten different channels of reverb spread out into the different speakers, with different delays, contouring, reverb times—to make one reverb."

One scene, in particular, stands out. It's Mangini's favorite sound moment, though he had nothing to do with it. Gaston, the rival for Belle's affection, has stormed the castle to kill the Beast. Gaston and the Beast are outdoors in a second-story courtyard, with thunder, lightning and rain cascading all around. Gaston yells for the Beast to show himself, and his voice becomes an eerie, operatic tenor, bouncing off the walls, so that for a moment, you ask, "Is he inside or outside?" Porter reveals that the effect was more than a slap delay:

"That's a combination. I used both Eventides to get four separated delays, and then I sent each of those through my 480 and Quantec to pick up reverbs on the delays. I used the 200 to pick up a really thin reverb on the dry voice. On the 480, you can get secondary delays within the reverb. So the main component is the delay, but with each delay there are secondary delays with reverb on them. Definitively, with the effects and music in the scene, you hear the slap. But a dry slap wouldn't sound right. The combination smooths the slaps out and elongates them.

"Again, that one is sent out left-center-right-surround, with a very large delay reverb in the surrounds so that it trails out behind you with each delivery of the line. That always helps to keep the focus on the screen. I find that when I go into surrounds with reverb, it's best to keep the delay quite a bit away from the front screen. The last thing you want is to hear something in the surrounds preceding the front screen, especially if you're in the back of the theater. Very distracting. But you don't notice it if it's a far enough delay behind the screen—it becomes part of the ambience."

"He's one of the few mixers who likes tasty, unique reverbs in every

Executive producer/lyricist Howard Ashman, orchestrator Danny Troob and composer Alan Menken (left to right)

scene," Mangini says of Porter. "He not only loves to ride reverbs, he loves to work those delays and ride them through a scene. He loves to ride EQ as a character turns. In animation, you record the voice on-mic, up-front. But Terry will put that live recording quality back into it—you know, if somebody turns off-mic, he'll roll off a little top, roll off a little bottom. The character turns back on-mic and he puts that curve back into it. He gives it a live-action feel, which creates that verisimilitude you need to help sell something that's such an artifice, which is a cartoon."

Actually, cartoon is a no-no word on the Disney lot, and this animated film feels nothing like Saturday morning. Part of that is because most of the animated characters in *Beauty* are human-based—no anthropomorphic dogs here (though there are anthropomorphized tea pots and dinnerware). Furthermore, studio head Jeffrey Katzenberg wants to move away from previous Disney projects, which called for very few effects, and toward a live-action soundtrack. The seam that holds the two eras together is the traditional Disney music. And in *Beauty*, the music is stunning.

Original Score Recording

Beauty and the Beast is wall-to-wall music. You never really get away from it—six songs and a beautiful, melodic, pastoral underscore. The songs were recorded in New York City with a 65-piece orchestra (mostly from the New York Philharmonic) at BMG's Studio A, mixed by Mike Farrow. The underscore was recorded on the Radford stage at the Sony lot (formerly the MGM lot) in Culver City, Calif., and mixed by John Richards at Evergreen in Burbank. Overseeing the 18-month process was music editor Kathleen Bennett.

"This film is the music," Bennett says, "and I know I say that from a biased viewpoint, but it truly is built around the songs. They are integral to the story."

All songs were recorded well in advance of final picture, as storyboards and pencil tests were coming together. The orchestra came in first and recorded to a Mitsubishi 32-track digital machine. Vocalists came in for overdubs. When the songs called for a choir, such as "Belle," the opening number, or "The Mob Song," a 24-track vocal slave was added for appropriate size. The 16-voice choir was doubled and sometimes tripled when action called for the whole town to sing. Then everything was remixed to 24-track analog with Dolby SR.

"On the 24-track, we had three channels of left-center-right orchestra, with all the vocals separate," Bennett explains. "Because the process was so long, many times over the past year the people in editorial had to pull mag from that 24-track. So we tried to mix it into a configuration that was going to be useful for any purpose.

"Another one of my jobs," she continues, "was to provide editorial/animation staff with a variable click tempo for what are known as beat readings. That's how they determine where a particular action should take place. I got part of that information from the 24-track. We recorded all of the songs free-time, so after we recorded I had to build a variable click track for all the songs. It also helped in case we wanted to go back in later and sweeten a particular character movement with harp gliss or a horn blat on the orchestra track. We did this extensively on *Little Mermaid*, and this is where I learned to do it right, I think. On *Mermaid* I was provided with a final vocal track, laid against a scratch synth and piano track. I had to build a variable click track that we recorded the orchestra against. We then had final orchestra with final vocal, but it was like putting the cart before the horse."

The creepy forest that separates the town and castle is filled with plaintive baby cries and cat meows, slowed down to half- or quarter-speed, not to mention the wolf sounds, which are actually 90% pit bulls.

All transfers were made on the Disney lot, and Bennett arranged for song tracks to be delivered to editorial in various formats—single-stripe, full-coat, whatever—to fit all potential purposes. Editorial then took the tracks and cut rough animation to fit the music tracks in individual units.

"We had very little trouble in the final dub, just a little EQ," Bennett says, a sentiment echoed by music mixer Mel Metcalfe. "You'd never know that [the score and underscore] were recorded not only in two different places, but at two different times with two different orchestras and two different mixers."

"You go out whistling those songs and singing the lyrics," says Terry Porter. "And the whole feeling under the songs of keeping a live-action sound always underneath it is absolutely wonderful. That was done with the input of Mark and our effects mixer, Dave Hudson. There are no egos here. If music handles a moment just right, Dave is more than happy to pull the effects out. And if an effect is playing a moment right, Mel will make sure that he pulls the music back in the right spot. In animation, you can get away with not playing a real effect if the music is stinging something, where it just doesn't feel right in live action. That's what I love about animation: There are no rules."

"You have to look for the abstraction of the action as opposed to taking it literally," Mangini interjects. "That's true in all animated material because it's this make-believe world where you can do anything. It's a natural playground for sound nuts." ◑

The Hunt For Red October

HOLLYWOOD HAS ALWAYS REFLECTED public sentiment on the screen, and *The Hunt for Red October* was the first big film of the glasnost era to express the wave of disenchantment washing through the communist world. As Marko Ramius, Sean Connery gives voice to the Soviet Union's prize submarine captain who, with no remorse, deserts the government that deserted him. Given the pride of the Communist Party, defection was the deepest wound a Soviet officer could inflict. This time, the knife was 650 feet long and weighed 30,000 tons. Ramius' instrument of insurrection was Red October, the largest nuclear submarine in the world.

Along with enough firepower to destroy 200 cities, this submarine had one feature that captured attention in theaters and the Paramount soundstage: a silent drive. This propellerless propulsion system made it easy for Ramius to sneak across the Atlantic, but it was a challenge for us sound people: Here was a major film whose plot pivoted around sound.

Sound as The Unseen Actor

BY FRANK SERAFINE

Capturing the Real Thing

Authenticity was a chief concern for Paramount supervising sound editors Cecelia Hall and George Watters II, but accuracy alone does not excite audiences. *Red October* was filmmaking on a grand scale. It was in this "bigger than life" quality that Hall and Watters recognized the need for a sound team that could go "where no one has gone before." They called Alan Howarth and me, reuniting the team that created the warp drive stretch/suck/explosion for the U.S.S. Enterprise and other sounds for the *Star Trek* movies.

A lot of imagination would go into the making of *Red October*'s sound, but first we had to hear the real thing. John Paul Fasal traveled with Hall and Watters to Connecticut, where they spent a week on a nuclear submarine called The Shark. There, they were given free license by Capt. Russell Carr to record anything, except in some classified areas. Ron Patton and Bob Smith, representing a company called Sonalysts, were our consultants on all questions of naval authenticity. The Shark sessions yielded 45 1/4-inch stereo Nagra and DAT tapes.

The Navy was very cooperative. They fired "water slugs"—torpedo launches without the live ammunition—by flooding and pressurizing the torpedo tubes and then blowing them out with extremely high air pressure. The recordings testify to the power of this air release, which shook the entire sub. This sound came to be used for the countermeasures, which act as

Sean Connery (top) and
Alec Baldwin

torpedo decoys in the film by distracting the weapon from its homing path. The Shark recordings also helped with Foley. The crew ran different alarms and helped make periscope recordings. Every aspect of the various pieces of equipment was recorded: the periscope handles slapping up and down, the periscope rising and the sheath that goes around it.

> To connote the massive, water-displacing motion of the sub's propeller blades, I did cannon-balls off a diving board, which we captured from various acoustic perspectives.

Sonar: The Hunt for the Right Ping

Given the film's attention to visual detail and military authenticity, we couldn't just fill the soundtrack with the usual sonar blip or ASDIC pulse (as the British refer to it). We had to find high-tech sounds as distinctive as the movie's cutting-edge Navy look. Although the appropriate sonar wasn't in anyone's sound effects library, there was nothing inherently difficult about creating it ourselves. Howarth and Hall made an earlier attempt at some sonar pings with sine waves, to which director John McTiernan responded, "No, that's not it." It was extremely involved, as Hall remembers: "We must have created 500 different pings." Since he was familiar with the sound, Patton, a nuclear power plant consultant and submarine specialist, made some examples with an oscillator and a reverb unit to show us what real sonar sounded like. These, like many sounds, came close, but McTiernan believed we had yet to hit the target.

Early on, this search led to Hall's swimming pool, where we amplified various versions of sonar, put them through an underwater speaker at one end of the pool and re-recorded them from the other end, 42 feet away. This use of "nature's reverb" yielded the sonar sound for the little DSRV (Deep Submergence Rescue Vehicle), but finding the right pings for the big Russian and American subs took much longer.

Howarth's Synclavier proved useful for its ability to digitally recall previous EQ settings. Patton, Howarth and Fasal (who contributed a crucial sonar element) finally ran one of the sonar pings through an Eventide 949

Harmonizer along with many closely spaced delays from a Yamaha SPX90. When this sound was sampled into the Synclavier and played back at an interval just under a fifth, we found the Russian (and, later, American) pings. The resulting sound is heard when Red October is avoiding the homing torpedo in the rocky undersea channel known as Red Route One.

Once we had the exact sound we needed, the blips had to be synched to picture so the rate would increase as torpedoes and other objects came closer. Accomplishing this synchronization was not simply a matter of speeding up the ping tempo, especially in some of the suspenseful scenes. It had to have feeling, so instead of sequencing, Howarth turned to his Synclavier, which can provide the same accelerando but with a manual arpeggiator control for the subtle rate variation.

Finding the right sonar sound turned out to be an epic task that went on for months, but it was justified in terms of the believability and authenticity it added to the overall project.

The Blades

In the final theater mix, a flowing, watery sound comes from the front-left of the theater as we first glimpse the massive underbody of Dallas, the American sub. From the right-rear side of the theater, a lower, more aggressive pulsing sound promotes a feeling of traveling through water. The main sound elements used for this shot came from Howarth's recordings of tankers off Long Beach and the sounds I created in Hall's pool and in my studio. My job was to connote the massive, water-displacing motion of the propeller blades.

> Disneyland's massive air-conditioning turbines helped us create an effect that audiences would perceive as a nuclear reactor failure.

The tanker recordings were made with a Nagra recorder and balloon-covered mics. At depths of approximately 100 feet, these recordings picked up the higher frequency sounds associated with shaft rotation. Given the immense size of Dallas' propeller on the screen, we had to come up with something to represent these great surfaces twisting through the water. At Hall's pool, I did cannonballs off the diving board, which we captured from various acoustic perspectives. I built one mic by taping a Crown PZM capsule inside a 35mm film can. I filled it with 40-weight oil, then sealed it with epoxy and suspended it in the water. The oil can picked up the low-end sounds, and an air-can mic was used to capture higher frequencies. Several studio mics sealed in condoms were placed throughout the pool. A Crown SASS mic, placed just above the water, yielded additional ambience.

Once we had the sound we wanted, I slowed the cannonballs and triggered them rhythmically on an Emulator III so that one cannonball would equal one "rev" of the propeller blades. This "whooshing" sound was combined with a water-churning element from a paddle boat. Watters and Fasal added this effect, which contributed a "chugging" sound. On the soundstage, the large motor and shaft rotation sounds from the tanker sessions were merged with the paddle boat element and the watery sound of the prop blades as they muscle through the water. Together, these sounds fulfilled the technical and dramatic needs of this and many other exterior submarine shots.

Nuclear Reactor Failure

Back on dry land, I searched for the right sound for the nuclear reactor that powers the silent drive. I spent a full day making field recordings at Disneyland. The park's massive air-conditioning turbines helped us create an effect that audiences would perceive as a nuclear reactor failure. One of the world's largest air-conditioning facilities, these "chiller wind-ups," as they're called, cool the entire park. I used a Crown SASS and an Electro-Voice ND309 mic with my Technics DAT recorder to record the turbines.

Frank Serafine captures sounds at Disneyland.

Although I knew I had a useful sound from the start, it was important to record the sound from several perspectives. I walked around the units looking for the exact position where the mics could capture the "winding" at its gargantuan best. Once I had the raw sound, we layered it with other elements and slowed it down in time with the picture. In the theater, you hear a massive nuclear power failure. I used the Emulator III to access the field recordings from a Pinnacle 650MB read/write optical drive. With the E-III, I was able to decelerate the turbines to a halt, even though the original DAT recording never slowed from its steady, functioning status.

Imagined Ambience

"When the sound you don't find...put the mic in your mind." As we learned with our attempts to capture deep-ocean ambience, sometimes the "real thing" is not enough. Hall states, "Underwater ambience is very difficult. You have to make it up, because the actual ambience underwater is a rather unattractive, crackling sound that's there all the time. So you go down in the middle of the ocean and you get this—it sounds like telephone static—which is not very ominous and not very exciting. You have to invent it to match what people expect it to sound like."

Even when working on sound for a film with a strong reality base, you have to realize that people will not be going to see a documentary on nuclear submarines. Fantasy plays a part in all aspects of moviemaking, and sound is no exception to the rule. For every underwater shot, we needed an ominous ambience that places you deep below the ocean surface. Capturing this atmosphere was one of the goals of the Catalina Island session. At 150 feet, the mics picked up a tanker about five miles away, which was used for underwater ambience and as a background submarine presence. A closer-range recording of a tanker sitting idle was used as a submarine atmosphere for exterior shots.

About ten elements went into the underwater ambience, some of which came from slowed-down bubbles and water entering Hall's pool through a garden hose. Mixed with Basil Poledouris' powerful music, our deep-ocean ambience had to match and magnify the ominous character of the visuals and music. We had heard how real deep-sea sound lacked feeling, so we made our own. As McTiernan says, "You have to take license in movies because you are going for the emotion."

Bringing Emotion to Cold Steel

One particularly strong match between sound and picture occurred in the scene where Red October is traveling at 26 knots through Red Route One. As the ship's navigator daringly maneuvers past canyon walls and jutting ledges, the homing torpedo closes in furiously. The shot of the weapon heading straight at the camera is intense, and our job was to let it scream—to give it a war cry without losing authenticity.

The core element, as with all the other torpedoes, came from speedboat pass-bys at Lake Castaic. We needed an underwater character for the sound, something that had a propeller and a mechanical sound. An outboard motor seemed like a natural candidate. The nice thing about an outboard engine is that its gear case is immersed in water, with most of the engine above water. Fasal and Watters made underwater recordings of the boat passing by. Given the increased speed and range of sound underwater, the depth of the mics didn't seem to make much difference: As long as they were submerged several feet, they wouldn't pick up surface noise.

> There is an intense shot of a homing torpedo heading straight at the camera, and our job was to let it scream—to give it a war cry without losing authenticity.

They started recording from a stationary boat, but recordings made from a boat always pick up unwanted sounds like water slapping the bow. Fasal eventually recorded from shore, where he "waded way out into the water with someone holding onto my belt to help me balance an eight-foot boom extended out and a Nagra on my shoulder." He recalls how he made absolutely sure that he "didn't slip on the slimy rocks." Once again practicing "safe sound," we placed two condoms around each mic with a rubber band to seal the back.

Any time you put any membrane between the mic and the medium, you don't get the same frequency bias you would from a direct recording. Condoms work well because they emphasize certain frequecies, so a motor sounds like it's not from the surface, but from below. With all the reflections underwater, you get phase cancellations and boosts at certain frequencies. You have a lot of resonance. Since some frequencies build up and tend to resonate, it becomes tricky. But we got enough out of the Lake Castaic session that it became the basic element of the torpedo.

The final torpedo pass-by was sampled and pitch bent at Howarth's studio to give it a Doppler effect. This core element provided us with a foundation of credibility over which we could layer our "emotional sweeteners." Animal growls and shrieks, a Ferrari and a screeching screen door spring were added in to produce a torpedo sound that's credible but still seems to have a vengeful purpose of its own.

The DSRV Motors: Magnifying Reality

Typically, a film mix requires sounds that simply don't exist; often, our goal is to transform real sounds into something bigger than life. This was the nature of the work we did on the DSRV motors. At Hall's pool, we recorded a lot of submersible power tools and air drills for the motors. The script mentioned that the DSRV sub was going to be shown driving and maneuvering in various shots.

When you're doing field recording to gather raw sound material for that kind of sequence, you try to cover yourself by doing "starts," "stops" and "steadies." The resulting sounds were mixed with effects I had made when commissioned by the Pentagon to create sounds for the Army's new M1 tank operations simulator. The M1 and the DSRV share the acoustic characteristics that come with small, enclosed, metallic spaces. There were a lot of sounds to manage. I loaded all the field sounds from my Technics DAT onto the Pinnacle optical disk, where they could be stored in 16-bit stereo an hour at a time on my Dyaxis and brought up graphically on the Mac for editing. With more and more theaters installing high-quality sound systems, it is important to stay in the digital domain. The combination of all these elements is more dramatic than submersible motor sound, and yet it's entirely believable on-screen.

Supervising sound effects editors Cecelia Hall and George Watters II

Hull Stress Sounds

Through feedback from Ron Patton, we came up with ship stress sounds that communicated the shudderings and hull pops that a nuclear submarine goes through when diving or undergoing strong changes in momentum. Patton listened to a number of metal hits, knocks and scrapes, a variety of which came from my studio construction site and Disneyland recordings. He then picked out those closest to what he had heard on actual nuclear submarines. Having heard ship stress sounds over years of nuclear sub dives, he had specific characteristics in mind, and, in the end, we used only about ten hits out of 100.

The beauty of film sound is that it can sometimes have an even more subliminal effect on audiences than the music. In the dialog, Sean Connery and Alec Baldwin make the final statement on world peace while sharing a nostalgic longing for "the peace of fishing." For me, however, the last word goes to the serene lapping of water up the smooth hull of Red October as it mills up the flat Penobscot River in Maine. This is the unseen actor that closes the film without a word…just sound.⊙

Capturing Dialog For The Player

BY TOM KENNY

WHEN YOU THINK OF SPECIAL EFFECTS FILMS, you think George Lucas. When you think of music in films, you think Kubrick or Coppola. And when you think about dialog, it's Robert Altman. Foreground, background, traveling, multiple-source dialog—nobody does it better. And it ain't easy, either on the set or at the mix.

"We put mics everywhere and on everybody, and they go down on separate tracks," Altman says. "We use half-inch tape and two Otari 8-tracks, so we can have as many as 14 separate channels. Then that's all re-employed in the final mixing. I haven't done any looping in 20 years. I'll occasionally go in and add a line, but we don't even put looping deals in the actors' contracts."

No looping? In today's Hollywood? "Bob is committed to the idea of not looping—for any reason," says production sound mixer John Pritchett, who has worked with Altman on *Streamers*, *O.C. and Stiggs* and now *The Player*, a wry, often acerbic portrayal of behind-the-scenes Hollywood. "He believes the performance is compromised in a way that's not worth it. That's why he wants the option of gathering all these bits and pieces from the performance, rather than trying to get people to re-create."

Gathering those bits and pieces was Pritchett's job on *The Player*, and it involved as many as 15 mics (radio, boom and plant mics everywhere), two Sonosax mixers, two Otari MX-5050 8-tracks, phone taps, even a wireless monitoring system for Altman and others to hear what was going down to tape. The equipment all fits on "the largest sound cart ever made," measuring 6.5-feet-long by 5-feet-high by 28-inches-thick, "so it can still fit through a door."

During the shoot, Pritchett made a work-track mix down to a prototype Fostex PD-2 DAT machine for the picture editors (supervised by Geraldine Peroni). At the same time, Pritchett kept the seven open channels discrete (the eighth was for a 60Hz sync pulse) so that dialog levels could be varied in the final mix. Submixing was crucial to scenes such as the complex, *eight-minute* opening shot and the parties. Joel Shryack handled the submixing.

"We used one 8-track and two Sonosax mixers," Pritchett explains. "They're built with pre- and post-fader line outputs on each input. I had a large patch bay built by John Eldridge that allows me to feed the left-right-aux as submix buses into the first Sonosax, which goes straight to the multitrack. On the opening scene, we had 15 mics and only seven tracks. The mix that you see in the final is pretty close to what we did, but we wanted to give the post-production people handles on either end. Just because I'm fading mics out here and there doesn't mean they necessarily have to.

"When Bob edits," Pritchett continues, "he pulls individual tracks from the multitrack just to see what was there—to listen to conversations—and he may actually use the conversations in sync, but he may just pull them out and use them as extra sounds. The post people have to go back and figure out where everything is. It's a lot of material to sort through." (For Altman's next film, *L.A. Shortcuts*, Pritchett will use the PD-2's time code function, which not only gives him automatic cue points but allows post-production access to all tracks at any point through the use of an auto-assembly system.)

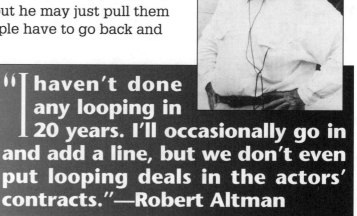

"I haven't done any looping in 20 years. I'll occasionally go in and add a line, but we don't even put looping deals in the actors' contracts."—Robert Altman

So many scenes in *The Player* involve complex dialog associations and, consequently, complex technical requirements: the voyeuristic phone calls (radio mics and a cellular phone tap), the restaurant scenes (plant mics and radio mics) and the parties. For Pritchett, the party at Sydney Pollack's house, where our hero first betrays his guilt, was the most difficult.

"We had all these very high-powered personalities, none of whom were given lines to say but almost all of whom were given microphones," he says. "We didn't know when they were going to appear, what they were going to say or what they were going to do. And the principals are carrying on a very quiet, confidential conversation, but they are wandering through all of these other conversations. We only had three hours to do it, because for them it was just a party. When the party was over, we were through shooting. It was a very short work day."

On to the final. Six weeks on the Otari Premiere in Stage 3 at Skywalker South (Santa Monica) with Matthew Iadarola on music and dialog, Stanley Kastner on effects. This is where the foreground/background dialog blend is created, with everything in balance.

"It's just the way music is done," Altman says. "You put a mic on all the instruments, isolate them as much as possible and do your mixing."

"I compare it to mixing a drum sound," Iadarola adds, "where you have all these channels of tom toms and snares and kick; they all make up a drum sound, but they have to be balanced against one another. If I have radio mics and booms for one shot, I have to EQ them all to sound natural. Then I have to do that all over again for the next shot. It isn't like you just open them up and they all play. Each shot needs tuning, which makes it more methodical in the mixing process."

Individual sound units were delivered to the dub stage on 3-band magnetic film. The film is not common three-stripe, as Iadarola points out, and it's rather unusual stock these days. "They did it that way so that they could use very traditional editing techniques of wiping and scraping with a razor blade," he says, "or wiping with an acetone, to get rid of pops and clicks while manipulating the sound mechanically. The drawback is that you only have three of the seven possible tracks. You have to select and then transfer at some point. I also had John [Pritchett's] DAT work track, which I used a lot of the time. His choices were very good in the mixdown."

Because everything comes in unlocked on separate tracks, there was quite a bit of flexibility in the final. Radio mics from Tram, Sanken and Lec-

So many scenes in *The Player* involve complex dialog associations and, consequently, complex technical requirements: the voyeuristic phone calls (radio mics and a cellular phone tap), the restaurant scenes (plant mics and radio mics) and the parties, which were actual parties with actual celebrities.

Griffin Mill (Tim Robbins) examines a threatening postcard.

tronsonics provided the isolation on the set (though Pritchett is quick to point out that they don't prevent bleeding; you can maintain acceptable bleeds as long as you obey the 3:1 rule), while booms from Neumann and Schoeps provide the ambience. Plant mics go everywhere, most notably on the tables in the restaurant scenes.

As on the set, the trickiest scenes for the mixers were the party scenes because of the visual shifts and constant introductions of new characters. Equally tricky, however, was a scene that takes place in a screening room, where Lily Tomlin and Scott Glenn appear onscreen, with the studio types watching from the seats and carrying on conversations.

"Everybody was untreated," Iadarola explains. "We had to try to create the feeling of their coming off the screen, in a screening room, with people talking to each other in the background about the screening, and people talking in the foreground, with all of it shifting. In terms of dialog texture, that was the most difficult and probably the most fun."

Sounds like a typical Altman film, if there is such a thing.⊙

Indiana Jones And The Last Crusade

For 80 DAYS DURING late 1988 and early 1989, an elite crew of sound technicians and craftsmen worked feverishly in a secluded rustic valley of Northern California to complete the mixing of the final segment of a trilogy of blockbuster films started nearly a decade before. For Sprocket Systems (the post-production division of Lucasfilm Ltd.), *Indiana Jones and the Last Crusade* was the culmination of work on the adventure series that began with *Raiders of the Lost Ark*.

DAT recorders and a Synclavier were put to use in recording effects tracks. Due to its superior generation-to-generation transfer capabilities, the Dolby SR (Spectral Recording) noise reduction system was used by the Sprocket Systems crew throughout the mixing, in what Summers says is the closest anyone is likely to get to a digital-quality, sprocketed film sound mixing system.

Unfortunately, Paramount Pictures, the film's distributor, decided not to release the film in SR because of logistical complications relating to the double-inventorying of release prints (the simultaneous distribution of the film in both SR-encoded and standard formats). However, in case the situation changed, the film's executive producer, George Lucas, had an SR master made.

An Interview With Gary Summers

BY NICHOLAS PASQUARIELLO

For sound designer Ben Burtt and dialog and re-recording mixer Gary Summers, who collaborated on the first two Indiana Jones films, working on the last of the series brought the challenge of creating a freshness to the track over and above what was achieved in the first two films of the series.

Summers, a veteran member of the Sprocket Systems team, was hired by Burtt in 1979 to work on *The Empire Strikes Back*. Since then he has mixed 13 features, as well as a host of special projects (such as the Disney/Lucas/Coppola collaboration, *Captain Eo*), IMAX films and TV shows. He was nominated for an Academy Award for Best Sound on *Return of the Jedi* in 1983.

❧　❧　❧

Mix: How did you approach the mixing of *The Last Crusade* soundtrack differently than the previous two Indiana Jones films?
Summers: We went into this film with the idea that this may be the last Indiana Jones film, and what are we going to do to satisfy ourselves creatively? How can we do something different on this one? Filmically, it's similar to the others in concept: There are chases and gunshots. Although

there's some neat and interesting stuff in this film, we were trying to figure out how we could add some shine to it, a little something around the edge.

Ben had his work cut out for him in coming up with sounds for the new material in the film, such as the vehicles, weapons and rats, etc. We also looked at technical considerations. We knew there would be a large release in the 70mm format. We'd done IMAX films, and I had done a film for Disney, *Captain Eo*—all using the stereo surround format—and we had a lot of fun creating that kind of environment.

We talked about creating stereo surrounds for Indiana Jones and went ahead with it in our creative planning. Then Paramount picked it up and said it was a great marketing device. [The second film in the series, *Indiana Jones and the Temple of Doom*, was done with just a mono surround channel.] The 70mm prints can be played in any 70mm theater because they are mono surround-compatible.

We could see from early screenings of the film that there were many opportunities for the stereo surrounds to be used effectively. That's when we coined the expression "Full Field, Split Surround." We felt it was different from other split surround films. The surround channels are always active, not just for isolated effects or music.

It's the sort of thing the audience may not always be aware of, and that's good! You don't want the sound to take people out of the picture; it should enhance, it should draw them further into the image.

Mix: Did you use the same format that was used on *Apocalypse Now* with respect to stereo surrounds?

Summers: Yes, it involves the six tracks of the 70mm print: left, center, right, surround and the two low-frequency enhancement channels. In designing this system, Dolby wanted to use stereo surrounds and still have the subwoofer channels. So they built an encoder box, which essentially is a series of lowpass and highpass filters. Tracks one, three and five are left, center, right, untouched and unfiltered. Track six is the mono surround channel in a conventional system, and in a split surround theater frequencies below 315 Hz are sent to left and right surround. Tracks two and four, below 100 Hz, go to the subwoofer channels in both types of theaters. Frequencies on tracks two and four above 315 Hz contain the stereo information for the split surrounds.

Mix: Did use of your Full Field, Split Surround technique affect the way you mixed your dialog?

Summers: It did, from a reverb standpoint. Most of the time I would add a separate stereo reverb to the stereo surrounds. The characters are often in caves or castles, and in those situations when someone yells, there's a great opportunity for the echo to be everywhere. So I put the stereo Quantec (QRS-XL) in the rear channels and used the Lexicon (224XL) across the front. From a creative standpoint, it was fun to do it that way.

There is some panning of dialog across the front channels. Ninety percent of the time the dialog will come out of the center speaker, but there are some shots—like the German staff car scene—where one guy's head is in the far corner, another guy's almost directly in the middle, one guy is walking alongside the truck, and they're all talking. The average 70mm screen is 45 to 50 feet across, and having all that dialog come out of the center channel seemed very strange, so we just panned the lines into the characters' mouths.

> "We went into this film with the idea that this may be the last Indiana Jones film, and what are we going to do to satisfy ourselves creatively?"
> —Gary Summers

You have to be very careful in those situations, because the audience is used to having it come out of the center speakers. If you notice that it's happening, you've got to fold it back in, because you don't want to shake people out of their seats. You don't want to make them aware of the soundtrack to the point that it distracts them from the experience as a whole.

Mix: How much of the final dialog track of *The Last Crusade* was looped for ADR?

Summers: About 25 percent, which is very low for our films. *Temple of Doom* was around 65 percent; *Willow* was 85 percent.

Mix: Why was there significantly less looping on the last Indiana Jones film?

Summers: A lot of the credit goes to Tony Dawe, the production recordist. Also the one thing that Steven [Spielberg, director] told me was to use production dialog at all costs, because that's the performance he liked.

Mix: Did you do a temporary mix?

Summers: When we work with George [Lucas], we always do very elaborate temp mixes for two reasons: First, it allows us to experiment with sound against the picture to see what things will work and what won't; second, it allows the director and the picture editors to begin to see the film closer to its final form. This aids them greatly in their task of telling the story. Even though it's a temp soundtrack and the music is not the real music, it begins to look and sound like a movie.

When we did the temp mix for *The Last Crusade* we were contemplating a stereo surround release, so it was an opportunity to try some creative experiments. We were quite pleased with the results, although we didn't

Dialog and re-recording mixer Gary Summers

get any direct feedback from Steven or George at that point, because they were preoccupied with the picture editing. John [Williams, the film's composer] also finds these temp mixes valuable, because it gives him a rough fingerprint of what types of musical moods work or don't work.

Mix: How much did Spielberg participate in the mix?

Summers: Steven was at the mix a total of six or seven days. Not a whole lot! I think this was greatly due to his previous trusting relationships with Ben and the rest of the crew working on the sound. He knew he didn't have to be there every minute to make decisions. We did all the premixing without the director there and had very few changes once he heard what we had done.

Once the premixing was done, Steven would fly up to look and listen. We previewed the first six (of the total of 14) reels for him, then we mixed them, and he came up the following week. We would preview the next eight reels for him and play him the reels we had already mixed. He would make his notes and changes for those reels, then we would implement those changes. After he left, we mixed the next eight reels, and when he came back up we screened those eight reels for him, after which he made some notes and changes.

Then we had a preview screening with an audience at the Northpoint Theater [in San Francisco]. After that screening they made myriad picture changes. It took about two weeks to incorporate all the changes into the soundtrack. We had a final screening for Steven here at the Ranch so he could give us the okay to begin making the final masters. ✎

Foley for Indy

David Slusser, Foley recordist for *Indiana Jones and the Last Crusade*, has been involved in recording, mixing and editing sound for film for over 15 years. He started at Lucasfilm eight years ago as an audio technician. He says that the successful recording of the Foley effects was a collaborative effort involving supervising sound editor Richard Hymns, who spotted the film; sound designer Ben Burtt; dialog and re-recording mixer Gary Summers; Foley editors Sandina Baillo and Jeannie Putnam; Foley artist Dennie Thorpe and himself.

All Foley work was done in the new Foley room at Skywalker Ranch in San Rafael, Calif. It was a real challenge on this film to make the Foley sounds compatible with Williams' soundtrack and Burtt's larger-than-life sound effects. "If you draw attention to the Foley, you're not doing a successful job, and yet you have to do something to get it to stand up to the other sound that's going on," says Slusser. Practically none of the production sound was used, in part because it was also going to be released in foreign language versions.

Slusser used a Schoeps mic for some of the Foley recording, but went to a special Neuman U87, modified by mic specialist Klaus Heyne, to produce a hotter signal with respect to the noise floor, which is rated at NC5. "We also saturated the tape and used Dolby SR with the SSL board," he says. As many as 22 separate mono tracks of Foley were recorded for certain scenes. Slusser recalls, "In some cases we used every track on the tape. We put SMPTE on track 24 and a 60Hz pilot tone on track 23 as a safety measure, in case we experienced problems locking to picture."

> "When we did rat footsteps, we used leather gloves, and I glued fake fingernails to the gloves to produce a realistic effect of rat scratching sounds on the casket. I whacked a wet chamois against a piece of concrete for when a rat falls on her shoulder." —David Slusser

To get the sound to work, Slusser made judicious use of compression to achieve a little more ringout—something that he says is not normally done in Foley work—and EQ to bring out the most recognizable aspects of a given sound. "In the case of footsteps in the cave," he explains, "for example, we also used some predelay so it sounded like they were actually recorded in a cave. For outside scenes we set up baffles in the room to absorb all reflections, and changed the pattern on the mic to make it more directional, thereby minimizing any reflections off the room walls." Any addition of reverb or other effects happened later, in the mixing stage.

"Sometimes we use very unconventional props to get the sounds; other times we go for the real thing," continues Slusser. "For example, we used real pottery to create sounds of breaking pottery. Or in a scene where one character drinks from the wrong cup and disintegrates, we found some old cow bones out on the Ranch property, and we used them to re-create his disintegration by shattering the bones on cobblestone."

It took about two weeks to record all the Foley effects for the film. The fast pace was possible due to several factors: The Foley room had been fine-tuned during a previous release, *Fletch Lives*, using the same team of people as on this release; and Foley artist Thorpe did her homework before she came into the studio, actually getting into the characters of the people she was working on to make the effects more convincing.

"She has an extensive set of props to get just the right set of sounds," Slusser notes. Thorpe, a veteran of more than 45 films, including *Indiana Jones and the Temple of Doom*, adds that often the process of creating the right sound is a matter of "pulling it out of the hat. For example, when we did rat footsteps, we used leather gloves, and I glued fake fingernails to the gloves to produce a realistic effect of rat scratching sounds on the casket. I whacked a wet chamois against a piece of concrete for when a rat falls on her shoulder." Thorpe claims to be most happy with the sound she created to accompany the brushing away of spider webs. "That's a tough one because it's an extremely quiet sound, but it has to get on tape. Someday I may say how I did it, but I'm not ready to say how I did it right now."

Regarding the use of digital techniques in Foley work, Slusser explains that for smaller video projects they sometimes make limited use of the Synclavier, but "for big-screen productions like this, we feel it's much more convincing to go with a live Foley performance."—*Paul Potyen*

The Abyss

THE CHEROKEE NUCLEAR POWER STATION outside Gaffney, S.C., is a long way from Hollywood. Abandoned after a local power company sank $700 million into construction, it sits deserted in the bleak, wintry landscape, its giant cooling pipes snaking away from the giant concrete containment tank like some alien life force.

"Yeah, the perfect place to shoot a movie like this," says director James Cameron of his project, *The Abyss,* the epic underwater adventure that stars Ed Harris, Mary Elizabeth Mastrantonio and Michael Biehn. Cameron holed up here along with producer Gale Anne Hurd, his cast and a crew of hundreds for over six months working on what production designer Leslie Dilley called "the most technologically advanced piece of filmmaking" at that time.

With 40% of the film's principal live-action photography taking place underwater, Cameron and Hurd's production company had to design and build experimental equipment and a commmunications system that would allow actors and the director to talk underwater and dialog to be recorded directly onto tape—for the first time ever—all before shooting a frame of film.

The complex underwater sequences were filmed in two specially constructed tanks. The first, A Tank, held 7.5 million gallons, was 55 feet deep and 209 feet across and was the world's largest fresh-water filtered tank. Additional scenes were shot in B Tank, which held 2.5 million gallons.

Sound Sinks To New Depths

BY IAIN BLAIR

"We'd originally planned to film on location in the Bahamas, where the story is set," Cameron says, "but we soon realized we had to have a totally controlled environment because of the large number of stunts and special effects involved.

"Underwater visibility was a major concern for me before we even started on the project properly," explains the director, who is an experienced diver. "In real life, deep-sea divers are used to working in total darkness, and therefore there's no need for them to be able to see very much out of their helmets. But for this film, I had to be able to see the actors' faces and hear their dialog."

To solve these problems, the company enlisted the expertise of Western Space & Marine, which designed and built ten experimental diving units for the film. In addition to engineering helmets that remain optically clear underwater, the company also installed state-of-the-art, aircraft-quality mics into each helmet. Then sound mixer and underwater communications designer Lee Orloff created a system for Cameron to talk to all the actors and technicians, whether they were underwater or on the surface.

Orloff, whose film and television credits include *Blood Simple, Starlight* and *Second Effort*, started by redesigning the aviation-style mics. "We split each mic onto a separate track so we could record each actor's dialog," he reports. "In all previous underwater films, this wasn't possible because of the conventional scuba breathing regulators. Our idea was to come up with

a system that would allow us to shoot as if we were on an ordinary sound-stage.

"It was also essential because Jim [Cameron] was directing underwater—another first in filmmaking," adds Orloff. "He was down in the tanks with all the actors for five hours at a time, filling up with air while still down there, so we had to wire the system to handle a number of layers of communication all at the same time."

Using a mixture of military equipment and commercial diving communications systems, then adapting and experimenting through trial and error, Orloff devised a system that permitted Cameron to communicate not only with the actors in the suits and submersibles, but also topside with his first assistant director and 20 crew members equipped with Clear-Com remote station headsets. In addition, all the crew members using Clear-Com intercoms could talk to each other.

Technical innovations on *The Abyss* were not confined solely to underwater filming and communications. The production also reached new heights—or depths—in terms of its sound design. While director Cameron

> The sound crew agreed that conventional hydrophone mics sounded horrible. Leyh began experimenting with different ways of waterproofing conventional mics, including encasing a Schoeps NK4 in a condom.

and his cast and crew splashed around in the tanks, supervising sound editor Dody Dorn and sound designer Blake Leyh were busy trying to complement the spectacular visuals with equally spectacular sound effects.

Both Dorn and Leyh are highly experienced (Dorn's credits include *The Big Chill*, *Silverado* and *Choose Me*, while Leyh's include *Under the Cherry Moon* and the special, edited version of Cameron's *Aliens*), and together they are responsible for the way *The Abyss* sounds.

"I concentrated on the actual sound design and effects, while Dody took care of all the dialog and ADR or looping," says Leyh. "The latter posed a special problem in post as it was all recorded underwater, so when we replaced any lines on the ADR soundstage, we had to use all the original

Sound designer Blake Leyh records the sound of a robot arm.

equipment, including the helmets and underwater mics."

Finding the right underwater mics was a special challenge for Leyh and sound effects recordist Dane Davis. "The first thing we all realized was that none of this had ever been done before," Leyh explains. "In the past it was always simple and sparse in terms of sound—a few bubbles and perhaps some underwater ambience. But when I first sat down with the director, he made it very clear that he wanted something totally different, and so the first few weeks of production were just spent figuring out how to do the job. We all agreed that conventional hydrophone mics sound horrible, and after some preliminary testing we decided to discard them altogether."

Leyh began experimenting with different ways of waterproofing conventional mics, and eventually hit on several solutions. "First we tried a Schoeps NK4 in a condom, and then a pair of PZM mics in a larger rubber enclosure, and finally some dynamic Sennheisers," he says. "It's an old trick, except that most people would probably use a cheap mic rather than a $1,200 Schoeps, which we actually tested 60 feet out in Santa Monica Bay one day. It died, but fortunately we managed to dry it out. We found that while this method worked quite well for some types of sounds, it also lacked high-end and detail because of the waterproofing process. So at that point we also started designing and developing our own mic, called the Aquaphone."

Leyh and Davis started from scratch, using an electret-condenser mic element waterproofed in such a way that its front plate was actually in contact with the water. "The big problem with hydraphones is that there's an intermediate conductor, so the sound has to go through a layer of epoxy before it reaches the diaphragm of the mic," explains Leyh. "But with the Aquaphone, there's no intermediate conductor, and the resulting sound is far superior. When we first started building it, we had no idea it would really perform, but it did, and we took it through various stages until we ended up with the Aquaphone MkIII. Everything was then recorded using that or conventional mics in rubbers. A lot of the time we also used multiple mics and combined the sounds."

Leyh and Davis recorded everything onto DAT using two Technics SVMD1 machines, often recording on them simultaneously. "Recording the real sounds in the film, such as the submersibles, the divers and some of the high-tech equipment like the remote-operated vehicles and robot arms was fairly straightforward," reports Leyh, "except that the DAT machines and the Schoeps mics were both highly susceptible to humidity—a bit of a problem on an underwater shoot."

Far more challenging was Leyh's job of recording the numerous special effects—"all the sounds that simply didn't exist, or that would have been impossible to record, such as an underwater avalanche or large sub crashing into the ocean floor," Leyh says. He came up with inventive solutions by experimenting with a wide array of raw materials as well as equipment. "One sound that worked really well involved dragging huge blocks of dry ice across steel girders and recording the results above water with a stereo pair of Schoeps and the PZMs. Another interesting find was recording fireworks both above and below water, as well as road flares. I also chanced across a table saw in the construction department, and that produced an unusual vibration. I recorded it with the Aquaphone, then slowed it down three octaves and used it as part of the nuclear sub's engine sound in conjunction with the other sampled sounds."

After they assembled most of the needed sound effects, Leyh and Dorn moved back to their Los Angeles studio to start on the huge amount of post-production involved; they were helped out by a team of 12 sound editors and assistants working under their direction. "We were sent the videotapes of various sequences as they were being rough-cut, and we started building up the soundtrack from that," Leyh explains. "All the different sounds we recorded were stored on DAT, and a lot of them were sampled on my Emulator III.

"For the rest of the post-production period, I went through every single sequence with a fine-toothed comb and figured out exactly what was needed sound-wise to complement what was happening onscreen."

To do this, Leyh used Professional Librarian and Sound Supervisor by Leonardo Software. "This had all the individual effects from my library neatly cataloged, so I could enter scenes from the film into the program, then list every sound I might have needed. These ended up being several thousand, and the software program was a great help in matching the effects in my library with the film effects in a very broad sense.

"It was a huge project, and it was also very frustrating at times," Leyh says. "There were many occasions where we spent hours and even days tinkering around with mics and experimenting with wiring. It was heartening to be on post-production where we could finally begin to hear some results from all the hard work."◉

> Leyh says it was a challenge to record "all the sounds that simply didn't exist, or that would have been impossible to record, such as an underwater avalanche or large sub crashing into the ocean floor. One sound that worked really well involved dragging huge blocks of dry ice across steel girders and recording the results above water with a stereo pair of Schoeps and the PZMs."

The Doors

The Music Is Your Special Friend: Sound Assembly For *The Doors*

BY TOM KENNY

THE DOORS IS NOT A ROCK 'N' ROLL MOVIE. Let's start there. It's a dramatic movie that contains more than two hours of music—Doors music—as underscore, as score, as performance, as narrative. Film reviews have labeled it a film about excess or a film about the '60s, and in many ways it is. But Wylie Stateman, co-supervising sound editor, says it best: "It's the 1960s the way you would want to remember them in the 1990s, which is in full-blown stereo with vibrant energy."

The Doors is a rock 'n' roll movie. It's about energy and passion. To the sound team on *The Doors*, that passion was translated into music, effects and dialog tracks that breathed and punched the spirit of the time, 1967-1971, pivotal years in the development of rock 'n' roll.

On a rainy night in Hollywood, the night before *The Doors* opened worldwide, a few key members of the sound crew assembled for a post-mortem rap in Paul Rothchild's home. Rothchild, the original Doors producer and music supervisor for the film, was joined by Bruce Botnick, orginal Doors engineer and music-premix/prerecord engineer on the film. Also, there were Stateman, Mike Minkler, supervising re-recording mixer and co-supervising sound editor, and Tim Claman, digital music systems supervisor and PostPro wizard. Budd Carr, executive music producer on the last five Oliver Stone films who handled administration and coordination, was absent.

"As with any Oliver Stone film, it was a collaborative effort," Rothchild says. "Everybody makes suggestions in everybody else's domain, and the good ones stick and the bad ones go. Oliver needed human interaction, sometimes from 8,000 people [in a crowd scene] and sometimes from five people in a studio."

"This was a love groove," says Stateman, referring to the slogan that was taped to the console throughout post-production. "It was a labor far beyond anybody coming into a daily job."

The film itself is immense. Minkler, who has mixed more than 200 films, including five of the top ten most expensive movies ever made, says, "This was the most difficult film I've ever mixed and the most enjoyable film I've ever mixed. There's so much going on that you can't get it all in one shot. If people want to examine this film and watch it ten times, I think they'll be pretty damn satisfied that we hit all the marks."

Sound crew collaboration began early in pre-production when the decision was made to record the live footage to multitrack. That meant location recordist Tod Maitland could carry actors separately, wouldn't have to mix and could open up space for ambience mics and onstage dialog. It also meant a hell of a lot of tracks in the final mix.

"Musical biographies have been done plenty of times in the past," Minkler says. "Everybody knows how to do it. You have a prerecord, you do a playback and then guys go out there and lip-sync."

"And then you write this retrospective piece," Stateman adds. "And that is *not* this movie."

Pre-production began with the problem of how to handle the live performance vocals: Should Val Kilmer, who plays Jim Morrison, lip-sync to Morrison's vocals, lip-sync to his own prerecorded vocals, or sing live on camera? This key decision would determine the music track assembly.

Kilmer, meanwhile, had sent Stone a rough video demo of himself doing Jim Morrison. Rothchild describes it as "an actor in cheap wig, cheap make-up, cheap camera, cheap lighting—performing Jim Morrison—singing the role." Stone knew Kilmer could do Morrison physically, that he had the moves. So when Rothchild told him that Kilmer was 80% of the way there on the voice, and that he could bring him up to 95%, Stone decided to test it.

Rothchild, Botnick and Kilmer went into Botnick's Hollywood studio, Digital Magnetics, to create new demos for "Back Door Man" and "Texas Radio & the Big Beat." One day Stone dropped by with the surviving members of The Doors. "I'll never forget this," Rothchild says. "We put up 'Texas Radio,' and about halfway through, John Densmore [Doors drummer] turned to me and said, 'Is that Jim, or is that Val?' And we cheered."

Stone still had to be convinced, however. Rothchild and Botnick took Nagra tapes of Kilmer lip-synching to Morrison and himself, and singing live, and transferred them to PCM-1610 digital 2-track, and matched music and voice to picture. They then transferred to mag and locked to picture, stereo format. "It was a primitive way of doing it in relation to the way it was actually done [in the film]," Botnick says. "But the technique was the same to the end."

Stone immediately saw that you couldn't have the famous Morrison vocal coming out of Kilmer's mouth and still be convincing. So he opted for live vocals, which was the choice all along of the sound crew. Basically, when you see Kilmer, you hear Kilmer. Otherwise it's Morrison. The resemblance is uncanny. The music is all original Doors, with a couple of brief exceptions.

Rothchild's task then was to fill Kilmer in on the nuances and idiosyncracies that made Morrison's vocals what they were. In that process, he says, "An equal amount of time was spent filling his cup with information on Jim's personality and psyche and motivations, so that when he hit the stage as a singer/actor, he wouldn't have to be relying so much on mimicking Jim as to digging inside of himself for the essence of Jim.

"The musician synchronization in this film is amazing," Rothchild adds. "The other three Doors actors had the impossible task of learning by rote the prerecorded work of The Doors, which was anywhere from 20 to 25 years old. Even The Doors couldn't resynchronize themselves to it. Every single note had to be learned because Oliver likes to shoot in 360—you never know where the camera is going to be. Each actor had to be prepared to be playing the tune perfectly at all times."

Each of the actors had an instrument coach, and each was supplied with a nightly "stringer" cassette of the next day's sequences. It was basically a Music Minus One—his part on the right, the mix on the left. These were put out daily and had to be re-edited according to Stone's changes.

Months prior to shooting, Rothchild and Botnick began designing a system for music playback and track assembly. They transferred the original Doors 4-track (first album) and 8-track masters carefully onto a Sony PCM-3324 digital 24-track. Then 24-track analog SR dubs were made with the same time code, referenced at 60 Hz. Kilmer overdubs and vocal comps were added for the concert songs/scenes, before transferring back to 3324 for pre-production and production editing.

For the set, Stone wanted to have every playback option available at any time, including the ability to use Morrison's or Kilmer's vocal track. "It occurred to us that we could use a Fostex 16-track," Botnick says, "and using a [TimeLine] Lynx synchronizer and the house composite sync generator, we could resolve the 16-track. We could provide playback in any magnitude of order because we had a mono composite mix. We had a separate drum track mix. We had separate bass, guitar, organ, Jim and Val.

"We would resolve the 16-track onstage, and the code would be transferred and jam-synched to an Otari 24-track with SR," he continues. "That 24-track was then resolved and transferred to mag for dailies." Dailies were handled by the staff at Soundelux, Stateman's facility, doing combine-mixdowns of six to eight different selected takes, in stereo.

If a shoot was to be handled differently the next day, edits were done overnight on the 3324. "On rare occasions," Rothchild remembers, "Oliver would say, 'I want to throw out that entire verse' in the middle of shooting. At that point it was 'Get out the blade, cut the 16-track, and pray.'"

"The Lynxes are smart enough that they rode right through the edits," Botnick adds. "What helped that also was the fact that since we were jam-synching brand-new code onto 24-track, it was continuous code." While the resolution stayed constant, different music appeared at the same time-code number for different days of the shoot and different takes of the same song. It was all lined up in post-production.

For the live vocal sequences, it had to be absolutely quiet on the set. There was no playback on the stage, no thundering rock 'n' roll for the audience. The actor-singers were set up with an earwig system, plastic flesh-colored inserts containing miniature, high-energy drivers for foldback. Prerecorded playback was sent to beltpack receivers, each with volume control. "We had standard recording studio earphone technology happening on this huge shoot," Rothchild says, "with different foldback to each performer."

Keyboards and guitar were not amplified, so keeping them quiet was no problem. Drums, however, had to be specially constructed. The snare, toms and kick were stuffed with foam rubber, and Zildjian supplied custom-built cymbals with top and bottom pieces of bronze and compressed foam in the middle.

To cover the likelihood of actor-drummer Kevin Dillon playing a passage that wasn't on the prerecorded track, each of the drums was set up with a piezo transducer, which triggered samples that were recorded onto the 24-track. "We could then sample John Densmore's toms and snare and come back with a drum part that was played perfectly to the eye," Rothchild says. "Even if it was played badly, it would work in the film."

Val Kilmer (left) and
Oliver Stone

The audiences, meanwhile, had to be loud and wild and crazy, but while Kilmer was singing they couldn't be fed music. Up until the camera roll, the song was being cranked out to the audience. When the scene started, it was replaced by a 30Hz tone called "Thumper." Essentially, Thumper was a hand-tapped click track (tapped into the 3324 by Rothchild's son Dan) that was filtered out in post-production. Since the music playback stopped just as the cameras began rolling, location recordist Tod Maitland was able to capture some of the finest audience tracks you'll hear. In many cases, the screams for "Light My Fire" and the like are the screams from the actual shoot, rather than ADR fly-ins.

After the shooting was finished, all of the music elements—prerecorded vocals (Kilmer's and Morrison's), production vocals and the original Doors tracks—were transferred D-to-D from the 3324 into a New England Digital PostPro. Archived and unreleased material was loaded in as well, including outtakes from the tour that produced the album *Absolutely Live*. The PostPro was locked to a KEM flatbed, both picture and music mag track, using the same setup as the film editors.

Rothchild, Tim Claman and music editor Carl Kaller then worked with the picture department, providing music for the temp dubs and making edits to fit selected takes. At the same time, they were comping production vocals that came in on Dolby SR 2-inch, and synchronizing the actor/musicians and the vocals—basically, assembling the premix.

"It was sort of like making a record on the live vocal performances that we had to build," Claman says. "We were collecting tiny little pieces of words and phrases from as many as two or three dozen live takes from dailies. We were constantly stretching and compressing—very minute surgery—to get the synchronization to work. We were trying to keep the energy of the live performance but picking the best performance to match it."

"[Tim] would take every single edit that we made, an instrument at a time, and he'd move the edit point," says Rothchild, who made his first window edit (manually, with meticulous, jigsaw-shaped splices) on The Doors' first album back in 1967. "He'd find the cleanest, sweetest spot for every instrument in that edit."

The music premix was not without its challenges, one of which was to sonically match the Kilmer and Morrison vocals, often within the same song. "In the song 'The End,' we originally had Val's vocal from beginning to end," Rothchild explains. "The first two verses are outside and inside the cave. Then at one point you go through the Indian's eye and…Bam! You're onstage at the Whisky a Go Go with Val singing the Jim part. I watched it

"We put up 'Texas Radio,' and about halfway through, John Densmore turned to me and said, 'Is that Jim, or is that Val?' And we cheered."
—Paul Rothchild

three times and said to Oliver, 'This doesn't work. If we're not looking at Val singing, we have to hear Jim.' It's the reverse of the other problem.

"But now we have a curious problem," he continues. "We have Jim's famous vocal 20 seconds away from Val's entrance onstage at the Whisky, in the same song. Fortunately, Val's performance is excellent. The original recording had a Sunset Sound live chamber on the take, so we couldn't take it off. We then had to match that echo to convince you psychologically that you're hearing the same person."

"On the original Jim vocal," Botnick adds, "it was an EMT 140 chamber with 15 ips slap—167 milliseconds. [On the final premix] we didn't have any EMTs, but we had these Lexicon 480Ls. And through fooling with EQ and adjusting the delays, we got it pretty much the same. It took a long time."

"But it was a very important point in the film," Rothchild cuts in. "At that moment you sell the whole idea of Val's voice."

The PostPro was then taken into the Cary Grant Theater on the Columbia lot, where all the music was mixed to three 6-track mag dubbers with SR, and back to the PostPro as well. "We basically had a master on the PostPro," Botnick says. "It had three tracks of our left-center-right, plus all the effects and reverb. We didn't marry them to our mix so that when it got to the dub stage, Michael could adjust it."

Claman was working completely with first-generation elements. And that's what was delivered to the dub stage at Skywalker Sound South for Mike Minkler, Wylie Stateman and Greg Landaker to mix. Botnick also provided underscore 3-tracks, which he converted from 2-track Doors originals using a Bedini Audio BASE processor. That way, Minkler had the option of lowering the vocal level when dialog appears onscreen.

While the PostPro was the workstation of choice for the disk-based music editing, any and all DAWs were used in the creation and manipulation of effects.

"Every piece of the latest, most sophisticated equipment was used on this film and exploited for its greatest attributes," Stateman says. "For the creation of transitional sounds and musical supporting sounds that had to be played along in tempo, we used the WaveFrame AudioFrame. We used the Synclavier 9600 for its abilities to sequence and task sounds out of RAM, where you need tremendous list management. And we used it for sound creation—camera flashes and some of the wind gusts that spin us in and out of sequences.

"And for developing the editorial work on the crowd scenes, we used the AMS AudioFile for its brute force," he continues. "Take a sound that's going to be repeated 750 times in one scene, cut it, then take another sound to lay over the top or to sweeten that particular effect with, run the list and spit it out to a 2-inch machine, Dolby SR."

Lexicon 480Ls were used for reverb and echo. Many of the effects had to be brought to their most mature point in the cutting room, long before the final mix. Sound editing was handled by Scott Gershin, Jay Richardson and Lon Bender at Soundelux.

The crowd scenes are memorable in this film largely because they're very real. Sure, there is some sweetening to add bulk, but the ambience and noise Tod Maitland gathered on the sets was used extensively in the final mix.

"After the edits were final," Minkler says, "Wylie went into the 5-track stereo recordings of these crowds, which have a reflection of the vocal, reflection of the music, but mostly crowds. They had great balance between them. We used them for ambience on the music as well. So when you see people in the audience, you feel them completely around you in 5-channel configuration—three in the front and two surround. You are in the middle of this concert."

Dialog editing took place at Soundelux and involved more than 2,000 hours of work. "There are lots of words in this picture," Minkler says. "We were up to 70 or 80 channels of dialog per reel, instead of the conventional five, six, seven or eight."

ADR was handled at Skywalker Sound South's "Bundy" annex (formerly Lion's Gate), while Gregg Orloff supervised the Foley mix from the new pit at the main facility.

True post-production began at Skywalker Sound South (Santa Monica, Calif.) on the newly installed Otari Premiere console in Dub Stage 1. It was the first feature film to pass through the facility. It's a THX monitoring environment, though KRK monitors were brought in as references, as they were used throughout the project.

"We had two objectives [in the recording]," Minkler says. "One was to supplement the reality, and the other was to enhance the non-reality and tell a story with it. The reality part has to be good and accurate and dramatic and fit in so you believe it. The other stuff is a lot of guesswork.

"During 'The End', for instance, the guys are all on acid and doing their thing, and we started introducing tons of sounds," he continues. "Paul started freaking out. 'What are you doing to my music?' Well, it was a palette. We came in with everything, and then started weeding and wading and playing."

On the dub stage, the three-man recording team basically had the 6-track mag reels, the production analog SR 24-track, a Synclavier and an AudioFrame. They continued to seek and receive input from their colleagues. "It was literally like building a house with five or six or eight people all giving input on how that house should look," Minkler says.

"There are nine people talking in a scene, and you have to hear every word," he continues. "And Paul wants to hear every lyric. And somebody else wants to hear every note of the bass. And somebody else wants to hear the guy talking in the background. We ended up where everybody was completely happy with the outcome, but, oh Manny, it made me old!"

The film was released in all major formats, with selected Cinema Digital Sound prints sent throughout the country. All were done at Skywalker, as were the transfers to optical.

"There's a lot of pictures and a lot of years at this table here tonight," Minkler says in summation. "We've all done gigantic projects as well as small ones, but certainly none of them have come up to this. Every foot of this film was rough. From dealing with the music on a file, dealing with the creativity of blending the dialog, effects and music together, premixing sound effects. Every single frame of every little element was so difficult because we pushed ourselves. That was the spirit of this film." ◔

TELEVISION

Mixing Without a Net

A Record Engineer's Guide To Mixing for Live Television

BY BOB CLEARMOUNTAIN

"**A**RE YOU OUT OF YOUR MIND? Why would I ever want to mix live television? There won't be enough time to get sounds! What if a mic goes dead? I can't deal with stage leakage! I could never handle not being able to rewind! I won't have enough control! It's all got to come out of a little TV speaker! What if something goes wrong?!"** These are a few of the paranoid excuses many record mixers manufacture to avoid live TV mixing. Unfortunately, those who maintain that attitude may never know what they're missing. They'll never feel that incredible adrenaline rush that comes with the knowledge that there are thousands, perhaps millions, of people hearing every fader move they make, and knowing there's no turning back once they're on the air. This may sound crazy, but once you get the bug, live broadcast mixing can become a serious addiction. Whether it's Live Aid, or cable television broadcasts for the Stones or The Who, or just a satellite radio show for Westwood One or DIR, I always find myself wishing the show would never end.

Now don't get me wrong, I certainly wouldn't have you believe it's all fun and games and nothing ever goes wrong. But problems can be minimized by some careful preparation, which is what this article is all about. With the right planning and a lot of cooperation and teamwork on the part of you and all the crews involved, the broadcast and the experience can be unforgettable. (That means good!)

Selecting a Mobile Audio Facility

If you're lucky, you'll have some control over which truck you'll use, so stay away from the likes of "Bubba's Van with Pans." Ask around. Try to get one of the top trucks that has experience with successful broadcasts and a reputation for good work. When checking out mobile facilities, keep in mind that a great crew is as important as working on a console you're comfortable with.

Get a stage input list from the P.A. company well ahead of time to make sure the mobile facility can handle the number of inputs you'll be dealing with. Allow a few to spare for last-minute additions and effects returns (such as delays) that you'll need to get your hands on. Don't forget to allot ten or 12 inputs for audience mics. Even though you might have 60 lines coming off the stage and audience, and the truck may only have a 40-input

Bob Clearmountain

mixing table, all the best trucks can supply an adequate additional mixer or
two to deal with the remaining lines efficiently.

Outboard Gear, Mics and DIs

Find out what outboard gear the truck has and make up a list of whatever
supplements you think you'll need. I wouldn't go hog wild with extra
stuff; you'll probably only have time to deal with one or two delays once
all hell breaks loose. Using things like external mic preamps is a nice
idea in the studio to obtain the best possible clarity and openness, but your
priority here should be to keep the signal paths as simple as possible to
limit the number of things that can go wrong. Two or three good digital reverbs ought to do just fine. If you can afford it, you might want to have at
least one extra of each type of gear; i.e., an extra compressor, reverb, delay,
etc., in case anything decides to pack up on you, or you realize after it's too
late that you need an extra effect on a particular song, which inevitably
happens.

The input list should tell you the mics and DIs the P.A. folks are using. If
it doesn't, make sure you obtain this information along with a list of the
mics and DIs that are available with the truck. Once you examine the mic
list, it'd be a good idea to get in touch with the house mixer and make
friends with him or her, so you can discuss any changes you may feel are
necessary. As you might imagine, this can be a touchy subject. If you're
dealing with a band that's already touring, try to catch a gig to hear what
the show sounds like from the audience, and perhaps take the house and
monitor mixers out for a drink if you can. I can't over-stress how important
it is to get these people on your side, especially when it comes to mic placement. Remember, if you're asking them to make compromises, you may
have to make a few yourself. If need be, you can double-mic some things
(put your own mics up next to theirs), but avoid that whenever possible to

> **D**on't go hog wild with extra equipment; you'll probably only have time to deal with one or two delays once all hell breaks loose.

The Sony 48-track DASH recorder

eliminate stage clutter and confusion during the show.

For the Rolling Stones cable broadcast from Atlantic City, the house mixer, Benji LaFevre, had worked out a rather unorthodox method of miking Charlie Watts' cymbals by placing two Neumann U87s directly above Charlie's head. (I guess this is why they're called "overheads.") Because Charlie sets his cymbals quite low, the wide-patterned U87s turned out to be almost as close to his stage monitor as they were to the cymbals. This arrangement was ideal for Benji but was hell for me. Adding two more cymbal mics would have looked quite cluttered on TV, so I had to make the compromise. With the help of some radical EQ, the cymbals sounded fine, and I think the overheads actually livened up the snare a bit. The monitor leakage was minimized by dipping most of the midrange out. This obviously was not an ideal solution, but it kept everyone happy...and it worked!

If there are more than one or two vocal mics on the stage, color code them with colored cloth tape so when band members approach a mic they're not normally on, you'll see it on the video monitor and be able to act accordingly. Color coding the appropriate channels on the console as well will let you respond quickly. If the show is a festival where stage setups are being changed, arrange with the house and monitor mixers for the vocal mics never to be unplugged throughout the show so the color-coding system doesn't get corrupted.

Miking the Audience

Most experienced mobile audio crews have worked out excellent methods of miking an audience, although it won't hurt to check on how it's been done. Obviously, the number of mics and placement will vary depending on the size of the venue. In an arena, for example, there should be at least eight to ten mics. A typical setup will usually consist of two shotguns on the sides of the stage aimed at the first few rows of the audience (usually the most enthusiastic), four mics (often condensers) hanging in the center and the back of the hall above the side loges, one on either side of the P.A./lighting platform, and either a stereo pair or a stereo mic at the back of the platform facing the back of the hall. Listen carefully to the different mics during the soundcheck.

You will notice that the mics toward the back of the hall sound delayed in relation to the ones nearer the stage. This is a result of the time sound takes to get from the stage to the far mics. For this reason it's a good idea to record the audience on four tracks, keeping the far mics as a separate pair from the close ones. This way, during the broadcast you can separately control the amount of delay that is tolerable, and in post-production the far tracks can be "pulled up," or dubbed onto a separate tape with time code and offset enough to get them in sync with the band. This permits them to be used at a higher level and helps a great deal when the audience is supposed to be clapping in time. Of course, if you're recording 24-track you probably won't want to devote four tracks to audience mics; balancing the mics will decrease delay annoyance.

Notes

Try to obtain a set list from the management of whomever is on the bill. If you're not already familiar with the artist(s), pick up copies of their records that contain the material they'll be playing. Listen to them attentively and take notes on solos, background vocals, etc. I've found a good format for these notes is to use a separate letter-size page for each song. Format each page with designated sections for intro, backing/featured vocals, solos, percussion, and so on, with a section for featured instruments such as the keyboard or guitar hook line. Leave enough room to add to this list later. If you're really lucky (and this is something you should push for), there will be a full rehearsal. Even better is to set up and do a practice run at a real gig prior to the night of the broadcast.

You'll probably be invited to record the show or rehearsal to multitrack as well. If so, talk the mobile facility crew into letting you rough mix those tapes on the afternoon before the broadcast. Besides giving you two runthroughs and a chance to update your notes, this is a good opportunity for you to go through the tapes and hear that everything is getting recorded properly.

Recording

Chances are you'll also be asked to record the show for possible post-production and rebroadcast. Budget permitting, I highly recommend recording digitally. The extremely low noise floor really helps when the band goes from a loud rocker to a soft ballad. Remember, your main focus during the show is the live mix, not the recording. At soundcheck you've got to set your levels for the loudest songs that will be played. You won't have time between songs for pushing mic faders up to optimize tape levels, you'll be too concerned with getting your mix ready for the next tune. If the producers can't afford digital, then Dolby SR is a must. If videotape will be rolling, you might want to avoid PD-format digital, because those machines don't seem to like being locked to anything, particularly video sync. In my opinion, the ultimate live recording medium is 48-track DASH digital.

Preparation

While studying the input, mic and equipment lists during the weeks before the show, stay in touch with the person who runs the remote recording truck. Keeping the truck's equipment in mind, lay out the console on paper. Figure out track assignments, monitor fader designations, effects sends and returns, and where all the mics will come up. Make a list of all the outboard gear you may need. Once you have this worked out as well as you can, get the information to the truck crew as soon as possible. (A fax machine will come in handy here.) They may want to make a modification or two to your plan. Heed their suggestions—they've done this before!

Hopefully the mixing table will have a "fader flip" mode so the small, or monitor, faders can be used for your mics and the large faders can be used for the mix. The advantage of this configuration is that you can set and forget your separate input levels to the multitrack on the small faders. The large faders, besides being easier to mix from, can have subgroups of things like drums and possibly percussion, keyboards, brass and audience to make your live mix easier. This makes doing the rough mix a snap. If you're using an external mixer, you can subgroup channels (for example, you might have a bunch of percussion mics coming up there) to a stereo pair patched to a couple of mix faders on the main board. Now you can also send them to individual tracks of the multitrack for flexibility in post-production. In addition, try to record the subgroup for your rough mix.

> This may sound a bit sneaky, but it won't hurt to have a good stereo audience loop handy in anticipation of any possible lulls in the show.

The Bird

You're probably going to want some assurance that after all your hard work your mix is actually getting through the satellite and to the listening (and viewing) audience intact. The way to accomplish this is to arrange for an "air monitor." This can consist of something as complex as a satellite downlink (a dish receiving the audio signal directly off the satellite that is connected to an external monitor switch on the console), or as simple as an FM tuner tuned to a local station simulcasting the show. Occasionally neither option is available, in which case you'll just have to hope for the best! Don't forget to set your VCR at home to tape the show! (I always forget.) If the satellite transmission company can't supply a downlink, chances are your truck crew can rig up a radio for you.

Communication

Be sure good communication has been set up with all the crews involved. The TV crew will usually supply an intercom from their control room so you can hear any necessary cues from the director. This can also be an occasional source of amusement. Ask for a direct intercom to both the monitor and house mixers. Also, get a talk-back into the stage monitors so you can talk to the musicians directly during soundcheck. This should be used only when necessary, and only after the house and monitor mixers are done getting what they need from their soundcheck. Your mobile crew will have a person onstage, usually with a wireless intercom, to track down hums, buzzes, bad mics and cables.

Video

For a television broadcast, your audio crew will obtain a video feed from the TV crew. More than likely this will be the "line feed," or what the viewing audience will be seeing. If your truck has an extra video monitor (which most do) you can obtain an isolated feed (iso) from either a fairly wide shot of the whole stage to see who is coming and going, or an iso of whichever camera is covering the lead vocalist or featured instrumentalist. For a radio broadcast, the truck will probably have its own camera to put on stage so you can have some idea of what's going on. If there's a large keyboard rig or percussion setup and the truck has an extra camera, you might want to set the camera over it to see what's being played.

When you're recording digitally, record time code and be sure the digital machines are connected to composite sync from the video truck and their clock input selector is set to "ext." This could save you a great deal of hassle during post-production. If the tape machine happens to be a Sony 3324, make sure it has a "VCLK" board installed. This is an option that allows the machine to be locked to video sync. Most of them have it by now, but if the one you're using doesn't, it is rentable.

Samples?

This may sound a bit sneaky, but it won't hurt to have a good stereo audience loop handy in anticipation of any possible lulls in the show. Hopefully you won't need it. An Eventide H3000 with the sampler option, a Publison or any high-quality, phase-locked stereo sampler with a looping function can be helpful here.

Snare and bass drum samples are useful but dangerous. It can be tricky getting samples to trigger properly in a live situation. Only consider this if you feel it's absolutely necessary. Should you choose to go this route, don't use a MIDI-controlled sampler, because the MIDI delay will make the samples too late. Sneak the sample in underneath the live drum carefully, checking that the sampler isn't mistriggering or flamming with the original drum. Don't ask for trouble by taking the original out. Tom toms aren't worth bothering with— just mic them properly. Whatever you do, first be sure it all works at soundcheck!

The Rolling Stones cable broadcast from Atlantic City

The Night

By this time, you should have extensive notes for each song. The running order of the songs inevitably gets changed many times before the show, so update the final set list. (This is why your song notes should be on separate sheets.) Between mixing and watching the line feed for visual cues, I've found it extremely difficult to read notes during the show. The best way around this is to find someone with a loud voice to yell out cues for you. Before the show, go over the notes with the person; ascertain that he or she understands the directions and can read your handwriting. It helps if the assistant was present while you were writing the notes or, better yet, had the notes dictated to him or her.

Well, you're ready to go now. Don't get nervous. Relax and don't think about the possibly millions of people out there who will listen to your mix...You'll do just fine, heh-heh. Instead of sitting there in a cold sweat during the last half hour before you're on the air, make sure you're truly ready. Check that no one's turned off echo sends/returns, mics, monitor channels, EQs or anything else while chasing down hums and buzzes. See if your pans and faders are properly positioned for the opening number. Check that no outboard effects were bumped (opening with "Death Flange" instead of "Large Hall" on the lead vocal may be inappropriate) and that any delay or harmonizer settings are correct. If you're planning to use samples, be sure they're still loaded. Check that the desk is in "solo safe" mode, or find out which solo button interrupts the stereo mix and which doesn't. Does your assistant have the notes in the proper order, and is he or she fully awake? You may experience the desire for a drink to calm your nerves. Beware—alcohol will slow your reaction time and possibly lead to some missed cues. I suggest waiting at least until the show's over (if not forever).

The Mix

You're on the air! This is when the fun starts. All you have to do now is pay attention and mix your ass off. If a mic goes out or something starts buzzing or crackling, track the problem down as quickly as you can, and if it's not in the truck, get on the intercom or tell someone to tell your contact onstage what it is. If everyone has done their job carefully, nothing major will screw up, but there's usually something, so be prepared. And most importantly, don't lose your temper—it never helps!

Bob Clearmountain and
Robbie Robertson

I recommend monitoring at an average level on bookshelf speakers most of the time, occasionally switching to the big speakers and a small mono speaker. For a TV mix the mono speaker is crucial because, of course, this is what most of your audience will be listening to. If you've been able to get a downlink or air monitor feed, you'll hear what processing is being done at the transmitter. Luckily, in the U.S. there is an FCC regulation that prohibits satellite uplinks from doing any signal processing at all, other than peak limiting to protect the transmitter from any sudden bursts of signal, and that won't affect anything unless you let your mix level get out of hand. Unfortunately, this doesn't prevent local TV and radio stations from doing massive amounts of limiting to keep their signal strong. Using a bit of musical-sounding compression on your stereo mix output can help to minimize the damage. Don't do any critical rides while listening to a signal that's been to a satellite and back, because it will have been delayed about a half second. Only use it for an overall sound balance.

Mixing for TV is a bit different from mixing for records since very few people are listening on decent stereos. Avoid going for a big, deep bottom end—most people won't hear it. Make sure you can hear the bass and bass drum on that small mono speaker. You may have to roll off some low bottom and

add lower mids to compensate. Keep your mix mono-compatible—don't hard-pan anything to the extreme left or right. For some mysterious reason, reverb seems to diminish on TV, so you may want to make things slightly wetter than you would normally. Don't be afraid of those audience mics—part of your job is to make the home viewers feel like they're part of the live audience, so they should hear as much live reaction as possible without obscuring the music. Use the audience mics sparingly as an additional echo return during the songs to maintain a sense of the sound of the hall, then swell them smoothly when the audience is responding—between songs and during breakdowns.

For television, top priority should always be what is on the screen. If you and the director have done your homework, you'll both be featuring the same things most of the time. Don't be afraid to exaggerate lead vocals, solos or other featured elements. If the screen is filled with the front of a guitar, everyone's going to expect to hear it loud and clear (that is, as long as someone's playing it).

And in the End

Well, you've done it. Show's over, you've done a great job, had a marvelous time and now you're wondering why you're so depressed. This is completely normal after two to five (or sometimes, as in the case of Live Aid, 12) hours of constant adrenaline rush. So...I guess you'll just have to go find the party!◍

Video for Audio

BY TOM KENNY

Focusing On Formats

AUDIO STUDIOS GEARING UP for post-production hardly makes news, and many studios are looking for ways to find new business. But audio post work requires more than merely installing a video monitor and synchronizer. Specifically, studios must consider which video recorder formats they should offer in order to compete successfully.

The answers depend on the market. New York, Atlanta and San Francisco have seen a lot of D-2; industrials are still primarily Beta SP; and 1-inch still reigns as the broadcast distribution standard. Yet outfitting an audio room with all formats can be expensive. What, then, makes sense?

"I would like to see some stability in the marketplace," says Rick Elliker of Servisound. "I don't want to see D-3 [Panasonic's 1/2-inch format] come around next week, because it's impossible to keep up with all these new formats. Once you could buy a tape machine and run it for ten years. Now you're lucky if you get five out of a piece of equipment. Usually, it's more like three."

All those interviewed seem to agree with Dwight Cook's sentiments: "The key is to pull yourself away from the technology and not just buy a machine because it's new. You have to buy it because it makes sense business-wise. It's the same rationale we use for audio equipment."

ADVANTAGE AUDIO, Burbank
Bill Koepnick, president

Animation shows come in on 1-inch after the telecine, and we lay down to 3/4-inch. At the same time we print code on the multitrack and then build all the sound effects and Foley on the multitrack. If we are editing dialog and music for the shows, we do that in the Pro Tools system. Then when we mix, we sync up the Pro Tools system live and bring its outputs up to four faders downstairs in the dub stage, and mix everything in a bounce mix to the multitrack.

Our work decks are Sony VO-9800s. If somebody brings in a 3/4-inch, we'll often copy from one VO-9800 to another, while at the same time printing our own VITC stripe into it, inserting our own characters. That way we know the time code is good. VITC seems to be difficult for people. Our whole setup here is dependent on VITC. When we edit sounds, we're using VITC meters to capture time code. We use Cue Sheet and the Macintosh to control sampling devices, and we're using Cue Sheet to fire sounds from these machines. With VITC, you just hit one button and you have your time code number, you hit another button and you have your MIDI note, and you say "Thanks." It's a two-button process.

The stuff that comes to us on 1-inch seems to be the most solid. Film people often want to go to 3/4-inch, but we ask them to please provide 1-inch. Time code is generally in the right place, at the right level, and the audio is right. We have an Ampex VPR-6, so the audio quality is pretty good.

ARDENT TELEPRODUCTIONS, Memphis
John Wulff, senior video editor

We support 1-inch, Beta SP and D-2. We have three Sony DVR-10s. We try to keep everything in the digital domain. We distribute 1-inch, and that's really the only reason those machines stay around. A lot of people are taking things on Beta SP now, because the automated cart machines at the stations are Beta machines.

Clients are thrilled with D-2 because you get four nice, CD-quality audio tracks, and you have a read-before-write function, called pre-read, that allows you to layer. You just take the output, bring it up through your switcher, put something on top of it, feed it back into itself, and instead of feedback you get an extra layer.

D-3 is going to put a lot of people in the production business. But if I were to start from scratch, my acquisition format would be Betacam SP. You will find S-VHS and Hi-8 trying to make inroads into facilities, especially corporate rooms. But I think initially you have to maintain a certain amount of compatibility with the outside world. Plus [with Betacam SP] you'll have better luck if you're planning any audio sweetening, multitrack post sweetening and locking to SMPTE time code.

COOK SOUND AND PICTURE WORKS, Houston
Dwight Cook, president

Video is suffering, as is audio, with the different formats and the incompatibility. The ultimate audio format does not yet exist, and neither does the ultimate video. In our market right now, 1-inch is still the broadcast standard. Beta SP is still pretty much standard for industrials—it's more portable, it's got a good look to it, and it's got great sound if you buy the top-of-the-line machine.

We've not seen many requests for D-2, but we'll see as it grows. If you're going to spend $60,000 to $80,000 for a video machine, then you need to make sure you're going to use it. It's the same rationale we use for audio equipment. It's probably easier for a start-up facility to start with D-2 than it is to take your existing machines, worry about their use, and buy D-2 in addition.

When D-2 came out there was a client backlash, because people who put it in tried to charge more per hour for this ultimate format, and the clients didn't really see the big difference between it and 1-inch. Ninety-five percent of our requests are for 1-inch, so we lay it back here, and it goes out for dubs.

I would recommend that people find one or two other owner/operators they can pull opinions from. If they know XYZ put in a D-2 machine, find out

> "The key is to pull yourself away from the technology and buy a machine because it makes sense business-wise, not just because it's new."
> —Dwight Cook

Jim Hodson (left) and Bill Koepnick at Advantage Audio

why and if it's paying for itself. Find out what works in other markets. That's a little less threatening than calling the competition in your own town and saying, "What do you think? How do you price this? Is it paying for itself?"

CRAWFORD POST-PRODUCTION, Atlanta
Steve Davis, senior audio engineer

D-2 is overwhelmingly popular. We have more than 20 1-inch machines, yet we've found so much demand for D-2 that we now have nearly 20 D-2 machines, both Sony and Ampex. We wouldn't have invested that money without a big client demand for it.

One-inch is still the king as a distribution format because it's the safest thing to do, just like 7.5ips mono is the safest for audio tapes. But in post-production, people like D-2 because of the obvious technical advantages and the ability to build stack reels and submaster elements without generation loss. Even our more upscale corporate clients prefer to master to D-2. They'll bring in Beta sources and take their dub away on Beta, but they'll make a D-2 master for the highest NTSC-quality generation for pulling subsequent copies and so forth.

> "When an ad agency leaves here for a client meeting, they want to walk out with a couple of 3/4-inch and a couple of VHS dubs for viewing."
> —Jeff Roth

D-1 is becoming important to many clients because communications are becoming so much more international, and component digital video gives you an easy primary format to go to PAL, as well as NTSC and a lot of the computer graphics devices.

EVERGREEN, Burbank
Steve Bartkowicz, maintenance engineer
Kevin Erickson, studio manager

We are a music scoring house, one part of the post-production process. Normally for video scoring we work with the 3/4-inch format. The music editor on the show brings in a 3/4-inch workprint with the final picture cut. All we use is the time code. Usually conductors get their own video monitor, along with one or two in the control room.

Normally composers get the same 3/4-inch workprint that we get, so they're working with the same master time code. If they call up and ask where we want the time code, we tell them channel 2 and address track, in case you have a dropout. And a temp track and dialog on channel 1, for playback purposes only. Many times composers will request dialog in their headphone mix while recording.

A lot of composers [and/or music editors] like to change the music at the recording session, so many bring their computer setup with its streamer system and set up in the control room or out on the stage. We'll feed them direct video out of the VCR. We'll then take a video feed from the music editor and go back into our distribution system. Whatever comes out of the music editor's computer is on all the monitors in the house. That way they can change where streamers are, where cuts are, where certain punches are, whatever. We give them SMPTE time code out of the VCR so that the computers can lock to it.

Generally, we record to multitrack, although a lot of times it goes direct to 3-track stereo, placed on a 4-track with time code on channel 4, of course, which is regenerated from our synchronizer. Code off a videocassette is usually less than desirable. Regenerating from the SMPTE time code number off the videocassette is mandatory. It's saved us a couple of times.

FOCUSED AUDIO, San Francisco
Jeff Roth, owner/engineer

When you're working on documentaries and long-format projects, there isn't the pressure to have as many different video formats, because you do a layover at the beginning of the project, and even if it's only a weeklong project, you do a layback at the end. Or you may not even do a layback to video. You might make a video transfer to work to, but your final audio can often go directly from center-track time code 1/4-inch to an optical negative.

We currently work to 3/4-inch, and we do all of our laybacks out of house. But the nature of our work changed when [engineer] Jay Shilliday came over following the Editel San Francisco fire. Since more ad agencies are working in San Francisco, D-2 has become the format to work on. When an ad agency leaves here for a client meeting—where they're probably just going to get feedback, and they've already booked time for revisions—they want to walk out with a couple of 3/4-inch and a couple of VHS dubs for viewing. Unless you have the D-2 in-house, you can't just turn around and make those dubs concurrently with the layback. That really goes hand in hand with Jay and the AudioFile, because if people are working on the File, they want speed, and that goes for turnaround time on the dubs as well.

D-2 will soon be a permanent fixture here. We'll probably get a 1-inch, too. We need to outfit so we have every format anybody might walk in with. That would include Beta SP.

MASTER'S WORKSHOP, Rexdale, Ontario
Bob Predovich, VP, general manager

Master's Workshop

Within Magnetic Enterprises [a division of McLean-Hunter Communications that includes Master's Workshop], we have D-1, D-2, Beta SP, 3/4-inch, 1-inch, S-VHS— whatever you need. In our mixing theaters, we project RGB S-VHS onto a 20-foot screen. From a video hardware standpoint, we're looking at using laserdisc. Magnetic North is the only company in Canada, as far as I know, that has an Optical Disc Corporation recordable laserdisc machine. We support the EditDroid up here, Lucas' picture editing system, and it requires laserdiscs—standard, play-at-home laserdiscs.

Magnetic South has D-2; Magnetic North has D-1 and a number of 1-inch machines. A lot of people wonder if D-2 or D-3 is going to become the standard. I say the future is going to be component video, which is D-1. Whether the standard will be D-1 is hard to say. From a sound standpoint, facilities like ours would have to have relationships with companies like Magnetic North in order to tag onto D-1, be-

VIDEO FORMATS, BRIEFLY

	TAPE WIDTH	LINEAR TRACKS	PCM (DIGITAL) TRACKS	AFM TRACKS	DEDICATED TC TRACK?
3/4" U-Matic	3/4"	2	—	—	Yes*
VHS	1/2"	1-2	—	2*	No
S-VHS	1/2"	2	—	2	No
1" C Format (NTSC)	1"	3	2*	—	No
Betacam	1/2"	2	—	—	Yes
Betacam SP	1/2"	2	—	2	Yes
D-1 (component)	19mm	1	4	—	Yes
D-2 (composite)	19mm	1	4	—	Yes
D-3 (composite)	1/2"	1	4	—	Yes
M II	1/2"	2	—	2	Yes

Certain models only

cause it's prohibitively expensive. It's not the kind of thing you will see sound companies going into, but you will have to support it. Whether you have to support it directly, or through some digital interface from a DAT tape or whatever, is another story.

We also have two Sony layback machines here, and they're kept busy every day. The majority of soundtracks going out on video are on 1-inch. You get into a currency of the industry, and 1-inch is certainly an easy currency.

NATIONAL SOUND, NYC
Peter Fish, creative director

A lot of our broadcast clients are going D-2. The prime format (now on the downward curve) is 1-inch. CBS is using D-2 just for stereo. We don't find much call for the four channels in audio mixing yet. The four channels are for elements. The online people are going to stack soundtracks up for a post mix, using channels 3 and 4 much the same way as they would on Beta. It's not a mixing format, though we sometimes print M&E mixes on 1 and 2, or split-mixes on 3 and 4, for foreign language.

All the major formats have their value where price meets quality. There's a certain point where you would be crazy to master on D-2. If your picture quality doesn't demand digital and your sound quality doesn't demand digital, why pay the price? If I was setting up a room, I'd make video format decisions based on my market and nothing else. Look at the market and ask: "Is it 1-inch, Beta or a 3/4-inch market?" Then build your room accordingly. D-1 is a great format. Why it hasn't caught on, I'm not sure.

Because what we do here is so based on the NED PostPro/Synclavier system, at a certain level we don't really care what we lay back to. Our workstations are such that we can clean up any tracks that come in. And the layback format is really just a client preference. What excites me is not necessarily the format, it's the digital workstation approach to audio post, because that's where the real work gets done.

SERVISOUND, NYC
Rick Elliker, VP, director of operations

We support everything from VHS to D-2. We have Beta, 3/4-inch, 1-inch, D-2 and VHS (for client dubs). Our D-2 is a Sony DVR-10, a great machine, but three months later they put out the DVR-20 with flying erase heads and a different drive system. It's hard to keep up with these things when they're 60 grand a pop. We have a competitor next door who is just now thinking of buying a Beta machine.

A lot of clients like Beta because they can have a mix on the first two tracks, and they can have an English version on another. Or they can split it out and have a mix-plus and a mix-minus on the same tape. And you get a better picture than a BVU or a 3/4-inch. We'll have 15 Betas that are elements, and we just pop the machine online and drop it onto a 2-inch machine. Then we can lay back without an operator.

Clients still bring in multiple formats. We still see a lot of 1-inch. Not as much D-2 as I expected. I don't think people are really comfortable with D-2 yet. Maybe the cost is still too high in the editing portion of the job. The stuff that we're doing in D-2 is cable programming, the higher-end stuff where they have the budgets to edit in D-2.

SOUND TECHNIQUES, Boston
Chris Anderson, chief engineer

We have a Sony 3100 1-inch for our primary layback and to lay off of. We have two ScreenSound systems, and they both lock to the BVW-70 Betacam SP deck, which is our work deck. The ScreenSounds lock to that so much better, which also makes us compatible with a lot of the corporate stuff that's shot on Beta. It seems to be the format of choice for industrials. It's light, portable and decent quality.

But houses still master to 1-inch. I've talked to some video editors, and I guess with Beta it's a little tougher to anticipate what it's going to do to your audio. Sometimes you hear pops and glitches on your audio tracks as you try to do an audio edit. Two houses in town support D-2, but we have yet to see any business from there.

Right now we swap time on two decks, between a BVU-800 with address track and the BVW-70. We're looking for another 70, because the 3/4-inch isn't nearly as much fun.

TRIAD, Des Moines, Iowa
Richard Trump, president

We have a Sony VO-9850 3/4-inch machine. Most of the people who have 1-inch know that we don't have it. A number of clients would love to see us have it, but whether it would pay off in the life of 1-inch is hard to predict at this point. You really want to predict that there is long enough life *in your market* to pay off what you're doing.

Two of the video studios we work with have center-track time code machines, so a lot of the material goes out on 1/4-inch rather than our laying back to 3/4-inch.

Some people bring in Betacam to do transfers on the spot. We have had an outfit bring in a 1-inch portable. We got it lashed up, and they had tape that was already striped, so all we had to do was read their time code, lock our equipment to it, and lay it back. It's definitely clumsy, because those machines don't have all the "goes-intos" and "goes-outtas" that you want.

ZENITH/dB STUDIOS, Chicago
Ric Coken, sound supervisor

We have 1-inch, Beta SP, 3/4-inch and 1/2-inch—obviously, for scratch stuff. The most popular formats in Chicago right now are 1-inch and Beta SP. Beta SP is running rampant for corporate industrial and a lot of the film being posted video. Whether it's because they love it or because that's what the video houses have to supply them with is not for me to decide. I think there are tons of video houses with tons of Beta SP.

There is some demand in Chicago for D-2, but on the sound end, we see very little pressure for it. To me, D-2 seems to be pretty much a commercial application. I'm not sure the people in long-strand have the budget to support that type of technology. D-2 is on the incline, but it's not 50-50.

If an audio facility is going into video, you're going to have to go with one-step-back technology, which at this point is probably 1-inch and Beta SP. Then you go with what's current, which would be D-2. It would be silly to do anything else. You can't go straight into D-2; your overhead is going to swamp you with the amount of business you'd be able to suck in.

Manufacturers have a far bigger stronghold on the industry right now than any of the artists or craftsmen. You know that as soon as they introduce D-3, they'll be talking about D-4. There's nothing wrong with increasing quality; it's just that it's so hot and heavy that the capital is going to bury us.◕

Time Code Basics

T IME CODE IS A SYSTEM that allows accurate identification of each video frame on a tape by assigning every frame a unique number. Each frame of time code is made up of an 80-bit stream of digital data containing bits for hours, minutes, seconds and frames, as well as other information. There is a sync word at the beginning of each 80-bit group that identifies the start of a new frame. The time code signal is recorded longitudinally on videotape (except for vertical interval time code, mentioned later) and is a continuous, frequency-modulated signal that sounds like a dirty warble tone, much like an old-fashioned drum machine sync tone.

Time code comes in a variety of formats. SMPTE time code includes 30 frames per second, 30fps drop-frame, 29.97 fps and 29.97fps drop-frame. EBU (the European standard) time code formats are 24 and 25 fps. Each type is used for a certain purpose, and they are not interchangeable. Thirty-fps code is always used in conjunction with 24fps film shoots (unless otherwise specified) and is generally acceptable for audio post-production work, as long as audio leaving the studio for layback is locked to the same type of code that it came in with. In virtually all cases, this code will be 29.97 fps, which is used in video houses because the time code rate must match the video frame rate. (Bear in mind that video houses rarely need to consider which rate code they are using because the VTRs and time code generators are all locked to a common sync generator. Don't be surprised if your contact at a video house acts confused when the subject of time code rates comes up.)

Then again, while standard 29.97fps code is most common, in some cases it causes a problem with determining program length. Because the code runs at 29.97 fps but counts to an even 30, the result is a loss of 1.8 frame counts per actual minute of time. If standard 29.97fps code is used to determine program length, after one real-time hour the time code will read only 00:59:56:12 (59 minutes, 56 seconds, 12 frames). When the time code finally reaches the 01:00:00:00 count, the program is 3 seconds and 18 frames too long. In broadcast this is thoroughly unacceptable. Since the video frame rate really is 29.97 fps, it is necessary for the time code numbers to reflect the actual number of frames that have gone by in order to time programs accurately.

This is done with the aid of drop-frame time code. Drop-frame is a variation whereby certain frame numbers are dropped from the count, so that the final count is 01:00:00:00 at the end of each real-time hour. The drop-frame system eliminates the first two frames in every minute except the tens' minutes (0, 10, 20, etc.), thus reducing the count by the necessary 108 frames. Remember, drop-frame runs at the same rate as non-drop-frame code (either 30 or 29.97 fps); only the counting system is different.

From a video sweetening perspective, the use of drop-frame or non-drop code is relatively unimportant and will usually be determined during the

Sync or Swim

BY ERIC WENOCUR

COUNTING RATE (HZ)	COUNTING METHOD (FRAMES PER SECOND)	DISPLAYED TIME ACCURACY	APPLICATION
24	24	real time	Motion pictures and film
25	25	real time	EBU standard for European television
29.97*	29.97 drop***	real time	NTSC television
	29.97 non-drop****	0.1% slow	NTSC television
30.00**	30 drop***	0.1% fast	Very rare
	30 non-drop****	real time	Film sync

* 29.97: Generated by all "color television" sync generators (i.e., almost all sync generators built after 1970). This is the speed at which a "black burst" signal runs (not to be confused with "black & white"). It is a standard color signal with a "color of black." Use this as your standard frame rate unless you are an expert and have a reason not to.
** 30.00: Usually available only in "internal crystal mode" of a time code generator, or from antique (black & white) television sync generators. Don't use this non-standard speed unless you are an expert and have a good reason. This is sometimes used in conjunction with motion picture film systems.
*** Skips 108 frames/hour at regular intervals.
**** Many users prefer 30 (full frame) counting because no numbers skip in the counting sequence—even though the elapsed time accuracy is slightly different from real time.

video editing. However, any tapes that will be synchronized with a drop-frame master should also contain drop-frame code. This will eliminate a lot of confusion. Another complication to remember is that certain frame numbers do not exist when drop-frame is employed. Thus, if we ask a synchronizer to park the tape at 1:01:00:00, it will be unable to do so because this frame number is not on the tape. The count actually changes from 01:00:59:29 to 01:01:00:02. The lack of certain frames also complicates offset calculations. Most time-code generators and synchronizers can deal with drop-frame code without problems, but given a choice, it may be preferable to use non-drop to simplify manual time code calculations.

The other two time code formats, 24 and 25 fps, are used for film work and European television (PAL, in which video runs at 25 fps), respectively. My own recommendation for audio studios is to stick with 29.97fps code for all in-house work. This will avoid any possible problems that arise from mixing frame rates with the video houses. One such problem is that the tempo and absolute pitch of audio material locked to one rate of code will change if played back synchronized at the other rate. The difference is only .1% (1/10 of 1%), but it might cause trouble in certain situations (for example, synchronizing live MIDI instruments with the system, which will play the pitches stored in their sequencer regardless of speed changes of the master tape).

Handling Time Code

Time code is a relatively volatile signal in two ways. It has a lot of high-frequency content and seems to leak into everything, and it is easily degraded by dubbing. Time code should never be dubbed from any tape source without first being regenerated or restored. If this is not done, each generation of code will become less and less readable.

Regenerating is a process whereby the code leaving a tape is used to feed a time code reader that simultaneously drives a generator that makes new code. This new code is fresh and can be recorded again. Because regenerating uses a generator, the code that comes out is subject to the sync-frame rate that the generator is locked to. In the case of most smaller studio synchronizers, the generator will simply lock to the incoming code, and thus the regenerated code will be exactly the same rate as the original.

However, many units also allow the generator (or entire synchronizer) to lock to other sources of sync. This is where the utmost care must be taken. If the generator is inadvertently locked to the wrong source of sync, the new code will no longer be locked to the video or audio it was originally associated with. Instead, it will emerge at the rate that the generator is locked to. For this reason, the generator must always be locked to the reader when dubbing code (unless all equipment is locked to a common sync generator).

When striping or post-striping time code on an audio tape, the generator should be internally referenced to its own crystal (non-resolved mode, if the generator is part of a synchronizer), and the ATR should be recording at its internally determined speed.

Conversely, when time code is recorded on a videotape, the time code generator and the VTR must be locked together, so that each time code number corresponds to a video frame. This can be accomplished by referencing the generator to the VTR's video output. If they are not locked together, the time code will float in relation to the video, causing massive synchronizing problems.

Regenerating is often referred to as jam synching the time code, because the reader is jamming new numbers into the generator. The thing to be watchful of is whether or not the code is being duplicated frame-for-frame. In a momentary jam sync, the generator looks at the reader at the start of the transfer but then continues to count upward on its own, regardless of what comes out of the reader. This is used to replace time code that has been partially erased or has unwanted breaks in it. A continuous jam sync (called "transfer" by at least one synchronizer manufacturer) causes the generator to duplicate the reader exactly, even if the incoming code jumps or stops. This second method is generally used for dubbing of code during video sweetening.

> The link that keeps the audio/ video relationship intact is a time reference.

A simple alternative to regenerating is restoring the code. Restoring code electronically reshapes the time code signal so that the data bits are clearly defined. The process does not involve a generator and does not have the same inherent dangers. Some time code devices provide a restored code output, which can be used for dubbing code with little worry. Also, the time code output of most 1-inch, Betacam and digital VTRs is already regenerated internally and suitable for re-recording.

Time code should not be recorded at 0 VU on audio tracks of an ATR or VTR as it tends to crosstalk. Recommended levels are between -10 and -5 VU. Also be sure that any noise reduction is bypassed on the track being used for time code. Keep in mind that "time code present" indicators on many VTRs and ATRs actually detect the presence of any audio signal. If the light is on but there is still no time code reading, patch the code output into a speaker to see if the time code actually exists.

Lastly, a word about vertical interval time code. VITC is a signal that is recorded in the vertical interval on a videotape by the video heads; it is not a longitudinal signal. The usefulness of this method, besides saving an audio track, is that the time code can be read at very slow speeds—even when the tape is not moving at all—because the video heads are always moving (longitudinal code is innaccurate at very slow speeds). Hence it is excellent for locating and cueing up to exact points on the videotape, such as a sound effect "hit." VITC can be recorded on any videotape, but it requires a special generator and reader.

Using Time Code

There are a few commonly accepted practices in the video industry that should be adopted by audio studios when dealing with time code. All synchronizing devices require a few seconds to bring their transports up to speed and lock before the actual audio can be used. For this reason, there must be sufficient time code before the audio material to allow for the preroll time. That means that the standard audio practice of tight leadering between cuts does not work. There must be at least 10 seconds o magnetic tape, with time code, before each selection for adequate preroll— as much as 30 seconds might sometimes prove useful. And please, do your video colleagues a favor by applying this practice to any audio tapes going to video houses!

Another standard practice is that of starting actual program at the 01:00:00:00 (one-hour) count. Besides being neat and tidy, this avoids the possibility of crossing the 24-hour count during preroll, thus sending the transports screaming backward to find a number less than 00. In addition, i is wise to start the time code at about 00:58:00:00 (58 minutes) to allow two minutes for tone, slates and silence before the show.

In a related rule, time code on a given tape should always be ascending. If there is a point where the time code jumps backward (for example, at an edit), there will be some duplicate numbers on the tape that will confuse the synchronizer.

And speaking of edits, I do not recommend making razor blade edits anywhere on a time-coded tape during program material. While it is *possible* to make a frame-accurate splice, it's not easy. If any numbers are splice out of the code it may cause a speed glitch when synchronized or, worse yet, loss of lip sync after the edit.

Resolving and Synchronizing

Now that I've explained the fundamentals of time code and its relation to video, we should also discuss the time code's relation to the audio. Before sweetening, the audio from the video edit master is dubbed off and transferred to audio tapes. The premise here is that the finished audio will ultimately be laid back onto the videotape, so there must be a means of ensuring that the audio will remain in sync with the picture.

A Fostex synchronizer and controller

The link that keeps the audio/video relationship intact is a time reference. Recording audio with a known time reference is like marking it with the ticking of a clock to guide it to the correct speed whenever it is played. Different time references have particular rates of ticks per second. These include video-control track (59.94 ticks per second), time code frames (29.97 or 30), pilot-tone cycles (60) or film perforations (24). The key to successfully using a time reference to retain audio sync is that once the time reference and audio material are put in an established relationship, that relationship must never be changed from one generation to the next.

The method used to make tapes play at a speed determined by the time reference is known as resolving the tape speed. Resolving is the process of regulating a tape's playback speed so that the time reference from the tape matches the rate of an external time reference. The resolving device continually compares the time reference signal off the tape with the external reference and controls the tape playback speed (via the capstan) so that the two rates match exactly. This comparing/compensating feedback loop happens continuously, so the resolver always keeps the references locked together.

Resolving playback speed has the inherent property of compensating for speed deviations that may have occurred during recording. However, the main purpose of resolving is not to keep the absolute pitch of the audio correct but to ensure that the audio will remain in-sync with video, or with audio on another machine.

Unlike VTRs with control track, audio machines traditionally have no means of resolving their own speed; the ATR runs at a speed determined by an internal crystal or the AC line frequency regardless of the exact speed at which the tape was recorded. When set for 15 inches per second, the crystal provides a speed close enough to 15 ips for most audio work. However, when picture sync is involved, the long-term speed drift of two non-synchronized machines is not acceptable. Consequently, audio tapes must use time code as a time reference. For this reason, time code must be present on an audio tape for it to be run in sync with other tapes. The time code allows the ATR's playback speed to be resolved so that the audio remains in-sync with the picture. It also allows the tape to be synchronized with other transports and cued to an exact location repeatedly.

For resolving to take place, the capstan speed must be controlled by an external synchronizer, rather than the internal crystal. ATRs with this capability generally have some type of interal/external selector for capstan control. A simple synchronizer will run a slave transport in sync with a master transport by using the time code on both tapes. The synchronizer compares the time code from both machines and controls the slave transport's speed so that the slave time code is playing at the same rate as the master time code. Thus the slave tape is being resolved to the master time code. The actual speed of the master is not even an issue—within reason—since the slave will be precisely locked to it. Likewise, any variations in the master tape's speed will be followed by the slave.

During sweetening, tachometer (tach) pulses from the transports may be used by the synchronizer to roughly keep track of tape position when time code cannot be read (as with fastwinding). This is known as tach-pulse updating. But only the time code can be used to resolve the ATR's speed. This is because only the time code has the precise relationship to the audio necessary to retain sync with the picture.✇

> The key to successfully using a time reference to retain audio sync is that once the time reference and audio material are put in an established relationship, that relationship must never be changed from one generation to the next.

Posting The Simpsons

HOMER SIMPSON takes his job as the operator of some vague component at a nuclear power facility rather unseriously. Nonetheless, Springfield gets its electricity with few interruptions. If Homer were posting his own show, however, it just wouldn't get done. It takes more than doughnuts and a beer at Moe's to get through the audio on *The Simpsons*, Fox-TV's animated hit.

Mike Mendel and Joe Boucher are associate producers for the series' production company, Gracie Films. Mendel has been with the show throughout its run. Just listing the audio components of *The Simpsons* is enough to fill an article, but ironically, before the audio makes its way to an Otari 32-track digital deck, it starts out as the equivalent of an old radio comedy from 60 years ago: character voices done by actors and actresses in a half-moon converging on a bank of microphones (in this case Neumann U87s) at 20th Century Fox in Los Angeles. Parts are read in sequence from each week's scripts by talents such as Julie Kavner, who plays Marge Simpson.

All of the dialog is recorded to a single track of an Otari analog 4-track. (Mendel says that the plan is eventually to go to digital, probably onto some sort of hard disk workstation. "We need that kind of versatility," he notes. "We need to be able to store the audio dailies and call them up instantly. One of the producers will come in looking for one of Bart's 'Ay, carambas' from another season's show, for instance. So we have to put together some kind of instant-access library.") The 4-track tape with the dialog is then sent over to nearby Laser-Pacific in Burbank, where it's transferred onto a WORM laserdisc and offline-edited from a CMX edit list. "That creates the master audio reel," Mendel says; it is also on 4-track analog tape. "A lot of Hollywood sitcoms are going over to laserdisc for that sort of editing."

Hearing Voices

The voices on *The Simpsons* have as much to do with creating the show's charm as the rough edges of series creator Matt Groening's renderings and the writing staff's sardonic, sarcastic scripts. Kavner's raspy Marge, Dan Castellaneta's sweet-and-low-brow Homer define the character visuals. Guesting on *The Simpsons* is a Hollywood vogue, and Mendel says that what motivated a number of the guest stars such as Sting to accept the roles was prompting by their own children. "[Guest shots] energize the

How Not to Have A Cow

BY DAN DALEY

recording sessions," Groening told a reporter. "[The guests] realize how much fun we have ad-libbing, and they get into the spirit of it. I always thought that we would have access to big-name stars because it's a very easy job. There's no memorization of lines, no rehearsals, and you don't have to put on makeup or costumes."

Getting those guest voices for each week's show is a trip unto itself. Michael Jackson (whose voice appeared as that of a corpulent, white mental patient who had delusions about being…well, Michael Jackson) came into the studio himself to do his parts, which Mendel says caused attendance at the sessions to rise dramatically.

Other times, the audio crew goes on the road. Both Sting and Jackie Mason were recorded in New York, where Mendel has used The Hit Factory and BMG Studios for characterization recordings. When Kavner had to go to Toronto for a film shoot, co-executive producers Mike Reiss and Al Jean went with her and got her parts for the first nine episodes on tape. Mendel got an entire baseball team on audio tape, including Darryl Strawberry and Mike Scioscia, for an episode planned around the opening of the 1992 baseball season. For Mendel, an ex-New Yorker, that may have been the only useful aspect of the Dodgers leaving Brooklyn for Los Angeles.

If there's no studio around, then it's down to DAT, and Mendel says he's had a lot of luck using the Sony portable non-time code deck. "We used DAT when we went up to [basketball star] Magic Johnson's house in Bel Air to record his phone conversation with Homer," Mendel explains.

It's Only Rock 'n' Roll

Guests who not only spoke but also sang were Aerosmith, who became the house band at Moe's Tavern in one episode. Their dialog was recorded at their home base in Boston. Singer Steve Tyler recut some vocals, and new guitar and harmonica parts were done before remixing "Young

> The voices on *The Simpsons* have as much to do with creating the show's charm as the rough edges of series creator Matt Groening's renderings and the writing staff's sardonic, sarcastic scripts.

> "The audio on this show is a lot of fun. It goes through so many different stages and processes—and it's a full-time job—but you don't really feel like it's work." —Mike Mendel

Peter Baird (left) and Tony Friedman of Post Logic (Hollywood) work on *Simpsons'* ADR.

Lust" for the show. "Walk This Way" is also on the episode, running during the closing credits. Other past musical guests include Steve Allen and Beverly D'Angelo as country singer Lurleen Lumpkin.

Mendel stripes mag from the new analog 4-track master produced from the laserdisc, and a "pencil track"—a sort of frame-by-frame storyboard—is created for the audio, so the producers and writers can fine-tune the dialog before it goes to picture. Those mag tracks are what gets sent to the animators, many of whom are working in Korea, where the painstaking and labor-intensive work that still characterizes animation can be done less expensively. Mouth movements of characters are matched to the prerecorded dialog tracks.

Once the animation comes back home on 1-inch videotape, Mark McJimsey does the offline audio and video editing. A copy is made from the tape sped up by 10%; sections of the sped-up version are inserted at certain action points—for example, if the producers decide Bart should be moving out of the way of Homer's hand a bit more quickly. The audio for those segments is also sped up directly on a 4-track deck and reinserted where necessary.

Dialog is conformed on a Pro Disk system at Skywalker Sound South by Bobby Mackston, and ADR is recorded against picture at both Skywalker and Post Logic in Hollywood. Travis Powers does *The Simpsons* sound effects and Foley on a Synclavier at his personal studio. According to Mendel, Powers' Synclavier is sent directly to a 24-track analog deck through the Otari console at Skywalker as picture runs. As the various sound effects pass by, if one doesn't quite pass muster, Powers fires off new ones until everyone's satisfied.

Big Band Bart

While this is going on, composer Alf Clausen is working at Evergreen Studios with the 40-piece orchestra used to score most of the *The Simpsons*. "Every week the show gets a full score," Mendel says. "There are usually about 30 cues—starts and stops—for each episode." Occasionally, library music is used, and Clausen also provides other types of material, like rock tracks, for specific episodes. Composer Danny Elfman wrote and recorded the series' title music.

A dialog editor at Skywalker cuts individual tracks for each character, as well as new "walla" tracks (not quite dialog and not quite sound effects), and lays them along with stereo pair tracks of sound effects and music to the 24-track deck.

Once all of the elements have been assembled, they are mixed to a 32-track Otari digital recorder and finally laid back to picture at Digital Magic, located upstairs from Skywalker. "The audio comes up on tielines from downstairs and it's locked to picture upstairs," Mendel explains. *The Simp-*

sons is mixed in Dolby Surround and employs Dolby SR noise reduction.

The Simpsons is a success for a lot of reasons, many of which have yet to be truly understood. But it's Aerosmith's guest appearance on the show that perhaps best captures the core of the show's appeal: rude, innocent, loud, funny and without shame—all the same things that once made rock 'n' roll fun.

"The audio on this show is a lot of fun," Mendel concludes. "It goes through so many different stages and processes—and it's a full-time job—but you don't really feel like it's work."◔

Hollywood North

A NONDESCRIPT INDUSTRIAL WAREHOUSE in Redmond, Wash., 20 minutes (depending on traffic) from downtown Seattle, is home to the three main sets and physical production offices for the hit CBS-TV show *Northern Exposure*.

Northern Exposure began life as an eight-episode summer 1990 replacement series that was successful enough for CBS to order up more episodes for the 1991-92 season.

With a total of 14 Emmy Award nominations in 1991 and 1992, six Emmy Awards in '92 and numerous critical accolades, *Northern Exposure* is recognized as quality programming, with sound playing an important part.

The series takes place in the fictional town of Cicely, Alaska. The main indoor action takes place in the town tavern/restaurant, a well-appointed home in the woods and a funky lakeside cabin. These interior sets are the centerpiece of the warehouse in Redmond. They're surrounded by a maze of partial walls and props for the one-shot and occasionally appearing interior sets.

Turning an industrial warehouse into a soundstage required a few additions, including heavy sound-deadening door treatments, nursery mesh stretched across the roof (to cut down on rain noise) and lots of old carpets hung around the top of the cement walls to reduce the reverb time.

Eavesdropping On Northern Exposure

BY RICHARD MADDOX

The town of Roslyn, Wash. (population 860), stands in for the fictional town of Cicely. Roslyn is located more than two hours from Redmond, across Snoqualmie Pass on the eastern slope of the Cascade Mountains. Most exteriors are shot in and around the town, as are some interiors—the general store, the radio station and the waiting room for the doctor's office. It takes an average of four days to shoot the exteriors for one show, with the crew and actors staying in nearby Cle Elum for the duration.

The Production

Northern Exposure is an hour-long show, which means that about 44 minutes of actual program are needed for each episode. To get these 44 minutes ready to air on network TV takes almost $1.1 million and roughly eight weeks from start to finish.

The script is typically delivered two weeks before production begins. The production phase, when the program is actually filmed, takes about eight days (typically running 14 to 16 hours each) to shoot in and around Redmond and Roslyn.

The videotape editor has four days to assemble a cut of the show before the director fine-tunes it for another four days. The producers then take about a week to ten days to refine the director's cut. Once the executive producers (Joshua Brand and John Falsey) are happy, the picture is locked, and post-production audio work begins in earnest.

The cast of *Northern Exposure*

Audio post then takes another week or so to complete, typically finishing up the Thursday before air date. Since the show must be sent back to New York via satellite on Saturday morning, there is often a lot of midnight oil burning toward the end of post-production.

Sound Production

Two sound engineers (credited as production sound mixers in TV-land, even though most scenes are recorded using a single boom mic) trade off recording the show. Glenn Micallef, based out of Portland, Ore., and Bob Marts, a Seattle-based soundman who mainly does commercials and industrials, share the job. Marts, who's known Micallef for more than 12 years, did the first two shows as a boom operator and has since done some shows as the production mixer.

For TV/film audio engineers, most jobs are BYOG—bring your own gear. Both Micallef and Marts own fully stocked recording carts, which are rented to the show. The mixer also usually brings along his or her own boom operators as well. Becky Revak boom-ops for Micallef, and Paul Stroh boom-ops for Marts.

Micallef's and Marts' recording setup consists of an industry-standard

Sound effects for the show are most often original, field-recorded by the sound editors using a stereo DAT. Many car and truck sounds used in the show were recorded using Angarola's '64 Dodge Dart (its squeaking door sound is especially popular).

mono Nagra 4.2L, a Sonosax SX-S8 mixer and a full complement of mics (Schoeps are most often used) and wireless systems (Lectrosonics and Cetec Vega). Monitoring is handled by almost-industry-standard Sony MDR-V6 headphones. The equipment, all loaded onto a portable sound cart, is pretty typical for TV and film production.

A seemingly simple exterior scene of the main character, Joel (Rob Morrow), driving his truck into town is an example of what a mixer encounters on an exterior set. A hidden Schoeps 41 mic, clipped to the driver's sun visor, was used to record Joel talking to himself as he "drove" the truck. The truck was actually being pulled by a ShotMaker tow truck that held the camera crew and Marts. Marts was squeezed, with his equipment, into the cab of the ShotMaker truck.

The next scene, a close-up of Joel stopping the truck, saying his line and then driving off again, required remiking because a different truck was being used. Marts covered himself for this shot by putting a body mic on Morrow in addition to using a boom. Since the shot was through the passenger window, he didn't know if the boom could get in tight enough to get good sound beforehand. In the end, Marts used the boom mic over the body mic for the recording.

The dialog track must be kept as clean as possible since the show is also sent to MCA-TV/Universal (the distributor) as an M&E (music and effects only) for foreign sales. Multiple foreign languages can then be dubbed from the M&E master.

Ideally, every sound except for the dialog will be created during post-production. This includes subtle performance sounds such as utensil noises and chair and floor squeaks, as well as larger-scale sounds such as crowd noises, ambient effects, car engines and door slams. As in all analog recording, alignment/level tones (1 k and 10 k at -8 dB) must be laid down at the head of each new reel of tape (typically 3M 808). Each take must be well-documented on a take sheet as well as through a sound cue on the tape.

At "cut," the sound mixer notes whether the take was a keeper or not and may audition the take if any questionable sounds occurred. It's the mixer's responsibility to have pristine dialog tracks, letting the director know if another take is required for sound.

Rob Morrow plays Dr. Joel Fleischman.

Post-Production

With the 1991 season came a new location for post-production. Formerly done at Todd-AO, *Northern Exposure*'s audio home moved to Stage 4 at Skywalker Sound South in Santa Monica. Because it is completely digitally mixed in "CBS stereo surround" (i.e., Dolby Surround), *Northern Exposure* has some of the highest-quality TV sound available.

Supervising sound editor Bill Angarola oversees some of the best ears in the industry, including the re-recording team of Peter Cole (production dialog and ADR), Tony D'Amico

(Foley and music) and Gary Gegan (effects), who mix in a THX environment. Of course, their lives are simplified by the sound editors Miguel Rivera (dialog editor), Brian Risner (ADR editor) and Mike DePatti (sound effects editor), who clean up and prepare the sound for placement into the sound mix.

The film and audio tape from each day's production are sent down to L.A. for overnight processing. The film is developed and transferred to 1-inch videotape using a Rank Cintel telecine at Laser Pacific. The 1/4-inch audio tape is first transferred to 3/4-inch PCM format (Sony 1630). The PCM digital tape is used as the source for the audio transfer to the 1-inch videotape (called the daily reel). DAT backups are run at the same time.

Once production is complete, the videotape editor and the director work with the Montage system to develop their cuts. At this point, raw dialog tracks are used in sync with the picture. Music and sound effects locations then are spotted by associate producer Martin Bruestle and Angarola, although final decisions must be postponed until the producers do their final cut and the picture is locked.

Exteriors are shot in
Roslyn, Wash.

Music is an integral part of *Northern Exposure*. An audio framework for the show is formed by Cicely's AM radio station KBHR and its lone DJ, Chris (John Corbett). The station, used as background music in many scenes, certainly follows no known format, blending an eclectic mix of original artist show tunes, country, blues, jazz and rock. Transitional original music for the show is written by David Schwartz.

The show's theme song, also written by Schwartz, is a blend of Latin, Caribbean and Cajun rhythms and tonalities that fit perfectly with the funky in-the-middle-of-nowhere atmosphere of fictional Cicely. This feeling is carried over into Foley and sound effects as well, as the sound editing crew strives to sonically make the show sound rusty and a bit worn around the edges.

Dialog and FX

Once the picture is locked, a list of dialog replacement points and line additions are used to determine which actors have to come in for ADR supervising (Automated Dialog Replacement) or looping. Most ADR is done at the Music Source, a Seattle recording studio. Peter Barnes engineers the sessions, which typically last two days. For guest actors based in L.A., ADR is done at Skywalker.

Looping a line or word is necessary for three reasons: to accent the performance, to add off-camera or over-the-shoulder words or lines, or to cover a defect in the original production sound. Since executive producer Joshua Brand is also a writer, the majority of ADR is done to polish up and tie the scenes together through script additions.

ADR in Seattle is done using the AudioFile digital recording and editing system. Timing reference comes from a 3/4-inch videotape workprint with window time code. At the end of the looping session, the AudioFile edits

Ideally, every sound except for the dialog will be created during post-production. This includes subtle performance sounds such as utensil noises and chair and floor squeaks, as well as larger-scale sounds such as crowd noises, ambient effects, car engines and door slams.

are recorded onto 1/2-inch, 4-track tape with time code (1/4-inch and DAT safeties are also made). These are then sent down to Skywalker, where they are pieced together with the edited production dialog and transferred to the dialog 24-track.

Sound effects for the show are most often original, field-recorded by the sound editors using a stereo DAT, although standard sound effects sources are also used. As an example, many car and truck sounds used in the show were recorded using Angarola's '64 Dodge Dart (its squeaking door sound is especially popular).

It takes three analog 24-track machines using Dolby SR to hold all the bits of dialog, music and effects for the show. The 69 or so analog tracks, many of which are alternate sounds, music cuts and dialog, are submixed in groups (dialog, music, Foley, sound effects) onto a 32-track digital recorder. This becomes the master tape for the audio portion of the episode.

The final stereo mix is transferred to the edited 1-inch videotape master and to a D-2 master. A second pass, minus the dialog, is used to generate the M&E master tape.

You certainly won't find the weekly car chase/explosion/shootout sounds or the stock CD effects on *Northern Exposure.* You will, however, find a well-paced, atmospheric show that captures natural-world ambience through the use of the latest high-tech audio toys. If you find yourself getting caught up in the quirky goings-on of Cicely, Alaska, don't be surprised. After all, the dialog and acting are a complement to the sound production.◔

Handling *Northern Exposure* post-production at Skywalker Sound South is the team of (left to right) Miguel Rivera, Bill Angarola, Martin Bruestle, Gary Gegan, Peter Cole and Tony D'Amico.

Audio for The Wonder Years

OUND HAS TRADITIONALLY BEEN the poor relative of picture in television, but in recent years several shows have appeared that feature sound as an equal partner. Not surprisingly, these shows are usually innovative in other ways as well. *The Wonder Years* is a perfect example. It has met with critical acclaim, consistently placed high in the ratings, won a handful of awards (for writing, direction and quality programming) and garnered Emmy nominations for excellence in sound mixing.

Production and post-production are more highly interrelated on *The Wonder Years* than on many shows. Different stages of sound creation are overseen by different people, but sound plays an important role in the framework. Therefore, the show benefits tremendously from having a single, clear-cut purpose that serves as a litmus test for execution of everything from the most insignificant sound effect to picture edits: letting the audience into protagonist Kevin Arnold's head. "That's what we constantly convey to everyone who works for us, from the writers to the editors, because that's what makes the show different and special," says associate producer Bruce Nachbar, who oversees the audio post.

A second interesting aspect of the show is the use of the Montage cuts-only offline editing system, first introduced in 1984. The Montage is a non-linear, Betamax-driven machine that employs 17 SuperBeta decks and Bernoulli hard disks. The only information actually stored is time code and machine numbers, so nothing is printed until the final run.

Each episode of *The Wonder Years* begins with narrator Daniel Stern (*Diner*, *Breaking Away*, *Home Alone*, *City Slickers*), the adult Kevin Arnold, looking back on his childhood during the late '60s and early '70s. The show records to 24-track with 1/4-inch backup using a Neumann RSM 190 stereo mic. During the pilot, many mics were auditioned, and the Neumann was chosen because it had the right warmth for the stereo show.

Production dialog is recorded by production mixer Agamemnon "Aggie" Andrianos to 1/4-inch stereo Nagra in 2-track mono mode, primarily using Schoeps and Beyer microphones through a modified Sonosax mixer. Almost all scenes are boomed by operator Douglas Shamburger. When Shamburger and Andrianos use radio mics (frequently), they split the tracks and use one for the boom and the other for lavaliers, but, says Andrianos, "We always seem to settle on the boom track mixes." There are many two-camera set-

The Sound Of Nostalgia

BY AMY ZIFFER

The cast of *The Wonder Years*

ups in which each camera is given its own track. Andrianos' ultimate goal is to give post maximum control. "It takes a combination of set politics, hardware and good working techniques to get the job done," he asserts.

Whatever his formula, it works. About 90% of the dialog used in the final mix is from the production stage. "Aggie keeps production clean for us," Nachbar says. "I go with the school that says 'Use production as much as you can,' because you're going to get better performance and sound quality. The stage is not going to sound like the location where you shot, but there are instances when we need to change a line because something didn't come out clear or there's extraneous noise. We also try to keep looping to a minimum because we're dealing with kids. Their time is limited on the set, and we can't keep pulling them out of school to do ADR. First and foremost on the show, we care about the kids, and we have to take into account how everything we do will affect them."

Narration weaves in and out of the dialog, so timing is critical; because of its complexity, picture is cut to narration. Optimally, narration is done before shooting even starts so that it can be loaded into the Montage system, and when the dailies start coming in they can be cut together.

Only the highest-grade Beta tape is used on the Montage because of the stress induced from running back and forth. The show is loaded in by acts, and a series of monitors digitizes information so the operator can scroll to find the desired takes and scenes.

The online is done at Laser Pacific in Los Angeles as soon as time is available after the offline. The time code on the 3/4-inch generated by the Montage matches the 1-inch used in the online, so an edit decision list is generated from the latter, which has all the narration edits listed. That list is sent to West Productions, along with the 1/4-inch production dialog tapes and a 3/4-inch tape of stock footage used in each show. Dialog tracks used in the editorial process are transferred to 24-track with Dolby SR, and stock footage is used as the source for the sound of things like *The Newlywed Game*, Huntley and Brinkley news broadcasts, and Nixon speeches.

> "We go for a very realistic sound, but there can be those slight exaggerations to convey the point because that's how you hear and see things when you're 13 years old. You're a small person in this big world, and it's coming at you!"
> —Bruce Nachbar

Burbank-based West Productions does more than just dialog and sound effects editing for *The Wonder Years*; they also handle Foley, ADR, the final mix and layback. Nachbar enthusiastically endorses their work: "Dave [West] gives us wonderful Foley. We have the kids be very quiet during shooting, and we add everything in afterward, from car door slams to sneaker squeaks in the gym."

In cafeteria, hallway and other crowd scenes, the extras milling in the background are just mouthing their words, and walla is added later by a regular group of children supervised by Joyce Kurtz. One of her responsibilities is to keep an ear out for words like "dude" and "radical"— expressions that weren't around in 1970 and would not be authentic.

For sound design and assembly, West uses the WaveFrame Audio-Frame. "Being digital elevates the quality and gives us the speed to accommodate a fast turnaround and still be extremely creative," West says. "We can create new and different sound effects and interact with Bruce or Bob [Brush, executive producer] prior to the dubbing process."

While dialog editing is beginning, a spotting session will be held, attended by Nachbar, people from West Productions, composer J. Peter Robinson, music editor Don Sanders from Segue (known for *The Two Jakes* and other features), Bob Brush and producer/director Michael Dinner. Decisions about effects, music and ADR placement are made at the same time.

Stern and required actors are called back in for ADR to picture, which is generally done (including walla) in one day, and a spotting cassette is made for the composer. In past seasons, a Synclavier was used extensively for scoring. About two days before the mix, a music preview is put up, at which the composer notes suggestions to implement prior to the final mix.

In addition to the score, *The Wonder Years* relies heavily on source music. "Music instantly pulls you into a time and a mood," Nachbar explains, "and since our show takes place 20 years prior to the air date— that's the way we think of it—music is a very quick vehicle to [take you back to] what you were doing and what it felt like."

Most of the time, the masters they work with are regular commercial

Fred Savage plays Kevin Arnold

CDs, which are transferred to 4-track for the music editor to cut with. On occasion, vinyl records have been used, and the Prosonus NoNoise division (using the Sonic Solutions NoNoise system) has been used to remove clicks and pops.

One question that comes to mind is whether the rough quality of period recordings is as much a part of the memory of a musical selection as the music itself, and should be respected. "It depends on the episode," Nachbar says. "A lot of times the source music is working as score, so we want it to be clean. On other occasions, we're actually happy if it's a little dirty-sounding.

"The most important thing is that the music serve the mood of the show. Narration often takes precedence because that's what is truly leading us inside Kevin's head, and we don't want the distraction of clicks and pops."

A lot of music research is done with the editors going through old issues of *Billboard*, buying CDs and listening to hundreds of albums. In an episode called "Mom Wars," in which Kevin takes a big step away from dependence on his parents, the song "The Circle Game" was used to bring a lump to viewers' throats. It played over home movies of Kevin as a baby with his mom.

For reasons of integrity, there is one unbroken rule with regard to source music: no sound-alikes. "The composer has done versions of songs, on occasion," Nachbar remembers, "but not sound-alikes. Everybody remembers the original songs, and they pack so much emotion that you don't want to cheat anybody out of that moment. We deal with a lot of major artists, and a lot of times they say they don't want to sell to TV shows, but they'll sell to *The Wonder Years*. We don't get turned down."

When it comes to effects, the producers exercise some selectivity in deciding whether to go for effect or realism. "Basically, we're inside Kevin Arnold's head," Nachbar explains. "Nobody's dad is that mean, nobody's brother is that obnoxious, but when you're a little kid, your dad seems that mean sometimes and your brother seems like that much of a butthead. We're looking at life through Kevin's eyes and hearing it through his ears, so the sounds can be that much bigger.

"We go for a very realistic sound, but there can be those slight exaggerations to really convey the point, because that's how you hear and see things when you're 13 years old. You're a small person in this big world, and it's coming at you! We make that very clear with a preference for very strong sounds. The sound of his bicycle, for instance—the clicking of the chain. Kevin's bicycle is a three-speed, but it makes the sound of a ten-speed, because a three-speed doesn't make any sound. But who cares? You expect to hear the sound of a bicycle!"

In the mix there may be several stereo pairs of narration tracks, ADR, walla, effects, source music and score, with maybe a couple more 4-tracks for music and a cart machine, all being mixed to an interlocked 24-track. The mix begins early in the morning at West Productions, with Nachbar and Bob Brush previewing the show and making notes. Brush then leaves the stage, and Nachbar mixes the narration. Dave West runs the custom-degned, 120-input Neotek Encore theatrical stereo console, while his father, Academy and Emmy Award-winning Ray West, mixes effects. Music mixer John Mack completes the team.

After the first act is mixed, Brush is sent copy. While he's viewing it and making notes, the team goes on to the second act. Later that day, Brush returns with his notes, changes are made, act two is played back, and changes to it are made on the spot.

In the course of experimenting, the mix team has discovered some music techniques that transfer well to TV. "In 'Mom Wars,'" Nachbar recalls, "there's a scene where Kevin gets tackled in a football game. Reality is literally being driven home to him in slow motion, and we wanted to convey the fact that it's a big moment. Ken Topolsky, who's the producer and comes from a music background [he worked as music supervisor on *Flashdance* and *Witness*], said 'Why don't we try pre-fade echo?' It had a magnificent effect. It gave that hollow sound when you hear the grunts and groans and people hitting him.

"When we do a music slow-down—say, Kevin's listening to some song and he's really happy, and suddenly Becky Slater, his nemesis, appears in front of him—sometimes we use a Harmonizer and dial it in, but sometimes we just lean an arm into that 4-track. We'll do it both ways, depending on what's most effective."

The Wonder Years sound team

Over the years, the process has been honed down to where it now runs like clockwork. While one show is mixing, there are another two editing, maybe a third at the spotting and online stage, and a fourth shooting. "We've gotten into that groove where everybody knows what everybody wants," Nachbar says, "but you really have to keep on your toes and prioritize correctly. We try to schedule so we don't have two shows into sound post at the same time, because that would be too much for West to handle. So we spot one show after the other show is mixed. And there are hiatus weeks built in, because there are pre-empts throughout the season, so those keep things sane. Altogether, we do 24 episodes in a ten-month period."

Having ironed out the kinks means more attention this season is being given to subtleties, like backgrounds. Crickets, children playing outdoors, and occasional drive-bys in the street bring more life to a scene. Nachbar is now spending more time previewing effects, making sure everything's a go for the mix.

The system has worked well so far and will undoubtedly continue for the lifetime of the series. The show's creators were once quoted as having said that when disco comes in (in the show's 20-years-removed timeline), they'll take it off the air, because of a personal abhorrence for that style of music! But even now, while it's still on the air and exploring new ground, it's recognized as a show that has set new standards for its time.✎

Twin Peaks

THE VERY THOUGHT that David Lynch—the director of what was unquestionably the most twisted popular film of the '80s, *Blue Velvet*—could have made it to network TV with a series as weird as *Twin Peaks* boggles the mind. After all, this was the medium that gave us *America's Funniest Home Videos*, and Lynch didn't exactly have a track record with mainstream America. But occasionally something odd slips through the cracks and—surprise, surprise!—even becomes a hit. The *Twin Peaks* pilot was one of the most-watched programs of the season. Its success probably spurred hundreds of would-be rip-offs, each screenwriter trying for a story line more bizarre than the others. A lucky handful will make it into development, and one or two particularly rotten ones may even make it to the pilot stage. Why, it makes me proud to be an American!

Twin Peaks really *was* different from regular TV, in its characters, the way it looked, and even the way it sounded. The original two-hour pilot, directed by Lynch, was surely one of the most intriguing "TV movies" ever aired, and the world that was created—aurally and visually—formed the basis for the episodes that followed. So even though Lynch directed only a few other episodes, the series as a whole had a textural continuity that was in keeping with Lynch's original vision.

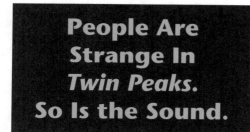

People Are Strange In *Twin Peaks*. So Is the Sound.

BY BLAIR JACKSON

Lynch was heavily involved in every aspect of the pilot, including the sound. According to Doug Murray, sound designer on that show, "David likes to keep an eye on everything that's going on, but at the same time, he gives people room to be creative. In the case of the sound, he certainly had some ideas that he vaguely sketched out to me, and there were a few instances where he had very specific ideas of what he wanted to hear, but he gave me a lot of latitude and was always open to new things. He told me that he liked the general style of the *Blue Velvet* [sound] track and asked me to emulate some of the things done in that film where appropriate, but I think most of what we ended up with was pretty original."

Lynch has worked with sound designer Alan Splet for most of his films; together they've forged a style that combines the use of unusual natural and machine noises, and music that is alternately lulling and jarringly melodramatic, into a strangely cohesive whole that inexplicably *works*. Lynch and Splet still work together, but for this TV project, Lynch chose Murray, an independent who works out of the San Francisco Bay Area's Saul Zaentz Film Center, to handle the sound chores. Murray's previous sound editor credits include the excellent "little" films *River's Edge* and *Smooth Talk*, and the big-budget hit *Colors*. "[The pilot] was a three-week cut and mix schedule," Murray says. "That's more than some TV schedules, but less than a conventional feature film. It was pretty intense.

"One of the things David likes is to take sound effects of machines and slow them way down to make almost musical textures out of them and mix

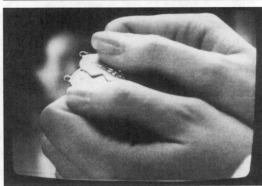
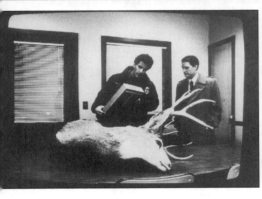

The many faces of *Twin Peaks*

them together in abstract ways to create backgrounds that have emotional impact the way music often does. I'd done a little of that sort of thing before, but most directors aren't interested in that direction."

No doubt about it, Lynch dares to be weird. For instance, to make the dream sequence as bizarre as possible, the actors actually spoke their lines and performed all their motions *backward*, and then the film was shown in reverse so it all looked and sounded "normal." Well, almost. But it's those odd, unexpected touches that Lynch and his crew come up with that make his work so memorable. I'm still haunted by scattered sounds and images from the pilot—the mournful ringing of a lone bell buoy, the grating, intermittent buzz of a defective light in the morgue, the horrifying blue-gray pallor of the victim's skin.

The sound effects Murray worked with came from a number of sources: Alan Splet's personal library of sounds ("David had a few specific ones he liked from previous films," Murray notes); sound libraries of other friends in the business; DAT recordings made on the show's Washington state locations by John Wentworth, who went on to be the post-production supervisor on the series; and recordings Murray made himself after seeing a rough cut of the pilot.

"I also used a couple of things from commercial sound effects libraries," Murray says, "but I prefer unique stuff." Murray used an Emulator III as his

primary tool and made extensive use of an Eventide Ultra-Harmonizer.

Wherever possible, Murray and his assistant Donny Blank (developer of Alchemy software, which they used as an editor, librarian and sound processing tool) did their own effects premixes. "That meant there were fewer choices when it came to the main mix, but it worked out very well," Murray says. "We had a Dyaxis, and it proved to be a very useful tool for mixing down and bouncing tracks. So we could lay down six tracks of sound, then mix down to the Dyaxis and lock that to picture and lay it back over to the multitrack recorder, which is an 8-track with six usable tracks because of the sync."

Since Angelo Badalamenti's music for the show was laid in after the effects were completed, Murray was unsure of how prominent his work would be until the final mix. "It was a little competitive," he admits. "I tried to get the effects so good that they would be featured instead of the music whenever possible.

"In the boxcar scene [an eerie, abandoned train that police investigators hypothesized was the murder site], the sound effects were very textural and musical in a way that was evocative of a train graveyard. I used slowed-down train whistles and train tracks rat-a-tat-tatting, and dogs and drips and all kinds of other sounds mixed in there, and it got used without any music at all. They went into the scene with music, then favored the effects, and then went out of it musically. It happened so seamlessly you didn't realize it wasn't one continuous flow of sound. It was all part of the 'musical score,' and it took you down to this deep, dark place."

> "David likes to take sound effects of machines and slow them down and mix them together in abstract ways to create backgrounds that have emotional impact."—Doug Murray

Director of the *Twin Peaks* pilot, David Lynch

The actual music in the pilot and the weekly series that followed was similarly unconventional. According to Murray, Badalamenti "created a number of themes, arranged them in different ways and recorded a lot of variations of the themes in different arrangements, with different tempos, different instrumentation. None of them had any hard sync reference to any scene in the movie, which is somewhat unusual.

"Then David and [music editor David] Slusser would cut from one arrangement to another during the course of a scene," Murray continues. "They would take a 24-track with different instruments on the separate tracks and mix down a selection into one possible arrangement. Then they'd try other combinations, so on one there might be guitar, drums and harmonica; on another, just strings and guitar. So there might be the same guitar part on these different variations on the theme, but the way the instruments were combined changed their effect on the scene. There were half a dozen different arrangements of the various themes at each tempo. I think it's the most unusual music I've ever heard on television."

Murray's involvement with *Twin Peaks* ended after the pilot, but it's fair to say that his sound work on that show established a mood that continued on the series, which was posted at Todd AO. "They didn't need to create a whole new world," he says of those who came after him, "because the world was already there. It's more like they explored the mansion we already built."

The Arsenio Hall Show

"LET'S...GET...BUSY!" chimes the rogue prince of late-night TV. With three lightning-quick orbits of an upraised, clenched hand, he coasts sideways, kickin' his house band, The Posse, with a subtle shimmy-shuffle. Arsenio's theme winds its way to multiple consoles via triple mult, Jensen three-way splitters.

Production mixer Gordon Klimuck pilots an Amek console like Buckaroo Bonzai, riding inputs and subgroups through an airborne audio rodeo. Coming out of a commercial, easing the attenuated Posse groove back to full gain, Klimuck prepares to open Arsenio's RF lavalier. The audio crew's steady patter of one-liners belies their focus: Each one is a joker and everyone is fair game. Their headsets, alive with brisk communication, give rise to an atmosphere of casual urgency and relaxed efficiency.

Guest band mixer Bart Chiate brings up the master faders on his Soundcraft 8000 console for Soul II Soul, ready to perform their hit single "Back To Life." Chiate, a veteran of live tours and recording projects, mixes the band live-to-videotape in stereo, with exceptionally high fidelity for television, typical of the trademark musical productions being turned out by the staff of *The Arsenio Hall Show*. No lip-synching, either: On *Arsenio* you either play *live*, or you don't play at all. It's an unusual phenomenon in an age of album-cloned performances, especially in front of a live audience and a viewing public accustomed to flawless audio for televised musical performances a la VH-1 and MTV.

A long list of major recording artists vie to play on this show. According to Chiate, the reason is a strong commitment on the part of the staff to the *listening* audience and to the acts themselves.

"Even though this is television," says Chiate, "we approach this purely from an audio perspective. We want the listeners to really get their money's worth. We take a lot of time scratching out levels, doing soundchecks and rehearsals. We pay attention to details and use plenty of inputs on the board to isolate and process individual sources. Also, we try to work with the artists and make certain *they're* happy with the sound. A lot of television audio people just don't take the time. That's the difference. We take the time."

A Peek Behind The Boards

BY BRAD LEIGH BENJAMIN

Arsenio with Goldie
Hawn

Getting Busy

The day starts at 9 a.m. with load-in of the guest band. For most acts, this procedure takes a couple of hours. But for Soul II Soul, an ensemble of 19 players and five dancers, basic setup and staging went well past noon. Boom operator Jim Braakenridge, fully familiar with the layout, works with the road crews, ensuring proper placement of gear and smooth communication between the roadies and the audio staff.

Audio technicians John Caswell and Jan Parent, whose primary responsibilities lie with the The Posse, also assist in guest band setup. Although their main objective is to oversee, maintain and configure The Posse stage's musical gear, they also supply supplemental gear to touring guest bands arriving without their full complement of instruments.

Floor A2 engineers Mark Weber and Pete San Filipo place and patch all guest band microphones. Later on they'll be responsible for placing production mics and hanging lavs on Arsenio and his guests.

All mic and direct lines on the set are divided into three groups or mults, consisting of house band lines, guest band lines and production mics. Each mult winds its way into a three-way splitter (with isolated Jensen transformers) designed by Jim Showker of Audiotek, L.A. The direct signal goes to the audio booth, the source of phantom power for those mics that require it. One split goes to the house P.A. mix position, and one goes to the stage monitor mix position.

Each mix position independently processes raw signal information. For the most part, the house band line, production mic levels and processing are fairly well dialed in. Levels, EQ and processing for the performing guests are set individually. One night, for instance, comedian Charles Fleischer (the voice of Roger Rabbit) did a rap tune with The Posse.

The major audio challenge lies in setting up the guest band within the scheduled timetable. Once the basic risers are in place and the drum kit is assembled, the process of scratching out levels begins. Bart Chiate, in communication via headset with house P.A. mixer Steve Anderson and stage monitor mixer David Velte, navigates this process from the audio booth.

Chairmen of the Boards

Adjacent to the main control room is the audio booth, domain of Klimuck and Chiate, who worked together on *Solid Gold*. Chiate prides himself on working effectively with the guest bands to get a sound that works for them and sounds good going out over the air. While a liaison between Chiate and the band is welcome, engineers are not permitted to come in and mix the bands themselves. However, Chiate is willing to take suggestions on relative levels, EQ, imaging and signal processing. He acknowledges that he's learned all sorts of live-mic and signal processing tricks from myriad producers, players and engineers who have worked with him in the booth.

Coordinating with Chiate for Soul II Soul was jazz/funk producer/engineer Frank Clark, a veteran of the L.A. film/TV soundtrack scene. Soul II Soul's leader, Jazzie B., and the band's musical director, Patrice Rushen, were in and out of the booth periodically, running ideas by Clark and Chiate.

Chiate's console, a Soundcraft 8000 32x8x2, is dedicated to guest bands. The master stereo outputs on this console are routed directly to two adjacent inputs on Klimuck's console, where Gordon has control of the show's overall mix. All guest bands are routed through Chiate's console. The only exceptions are single guest artists performing with The Posse, who require only a production mic input, or rap groups with little or no instrumentation. Rap groups are the only acts allowed to bring in prerecorded bed music, since that is an acknowledged part of the art form. They must, however, rap and scratch *live*—no sequenced vocals or effects.

Working with such a large ensemble, Chiate is usually maxed out on his inputs. Therefore, the mic signals from Soul II Soul's six violinists were routed directly to a 6-channel Yamaha M406 mixer and bused in stereo to two inputs of the Soundcraft 8000.

Chiate employs a variety of signal processors, including reverbs, delays, limiters, noise gates and a Harmonizer. Before the guest band arrives, he is already in possession of their CD. He auditions the tracks to be performed and dials in his effects accordingly. Effects receives are turned up a notch past where one thinks they sound good, because little details like reverb tend to get lost in broadcast.

For televised audio, Chiate must use an array of limiters while retaining dynamics in the sound. That's an art in itself. The extensive use of limiters during taping keeps the non-discriminating broadcast limiters (which affect the entire sum mix at the transmitter) out of the broadcast chain. Broadcast limiters pump, alias and do all sorts of nasty things that are distasteful to the home viewer/listener. By selectively limiting potential troublemaking sources, Chiate circumvents these problems.

His monitors are Yamaha NS-10s. Chiate sets up the mix in stereo but monitors in mono during the actual taping. He comments, "Eighty-five percent of our viewers receive the broadcast or listen in mono. Mono-monitored mixes sound better in stereo than vice versa, so we monitor in mono." While many of the show's affiliates broadcast in mono, the show is taped in full stereo, and plans are to go to a quad, Dolby surround format.

Klimuck's board is a custom-designed 56x24x2 Amek console from the 2500 Series. It has six sends and receives in each channel, 4-band paramet-

On *Arsenio* you either play live or you don't play at all. It's an unusual phenomenon in an age of lip-synched, album-cloned performances.

> **"We want the listeners to really get their money's worth. We take a lot of time scratching out levels, doing soundchecks and rehearsals."** —Bart Chiate

ric EQ and 11 grouping buses. It's wired for automation but Klimuck prefers to use it manually. Considering the live application, having the console remember where he *was* isn't nearly as important as having the console ergonomics expedite where he *is*.

Klimuck's console handles all the individual Posse line inputs, a stereo feed of the guest band from Chiate's Soundcraft 8000, all RF and hard-wired production mics, three stereo VTR machines, two Studer A10 1/4-inch stereo tape machines, and four cart machines (soon to be replaced by an Akai S1000 sampler). In addition, a rack-mount Yamaha M406 6-channel mixer handles all the Posse tom-tom and overhead mics, busing them down to two inputs on the Amek. Two additional Yamaha M406's are used as inputs for 12 Countryman Isomax audience reaction mics, bused down to two inputs on the Amek. Klimuck can adjust audience response signal levels with either the input faders or via a foot pedal located beneath the console when both hands are occupied. He monitors the overall mix on a pair of JBL 4345 mains, going to headphones only when the guest bands perform, enabling Chiate to get a clear listening perspective from his Yamaha NS-10s.

A multitude of cooling fans for 60 Varilights and five Super Trooper Xenon spots present the audio crew's most difficult challenge. The noise from the fans bleeds into the boom mic, which is frequently trained on Arsenio and his guest. To address this and other ambient problems, a signal processing chain, consisting of a notched Orban 672A active parametric EQ, a Brooke-Siren compressor/de-esser and a Cat 43 single-ended Dolby noise filter, is inserted into the boom's channel on the Amek.

Spread Out!

Above and behind the audience, at a 40x8x8 Yamaha PM3000 console, is Steve Anderson, mixing the sound for the house P.A. The Posse is premixed on an adjacent Amek console and bused to four of the Yamaha's eight subgroups, where they are processed through Anderson's EQ and outboard gear along with the console's production mic and guest band inputs. The audio fans out from the console through five outputs of an assignable matrix to six speaker locations.

Just off stage left, David Velte hovers over a Ramsa 840 40x18 console, part of a touring road system (unusually elaborate for television stage monitors). Velte sends six mixes to the house band and can send up to ten mixes to the guest band. The ten guest band mixes each go through their own Klark-Teknik EQ. Velte, working with the band's production liaison, always tries to take care of the players by setting the relative levels and EQ of each monitor to their exact specifications.

Audiotek's small wedge monitors are extremely effective for television. Director Sandi Fullerton likes them because they're visually unobtrusive. She also likes the EV 408 mics on the toms and overheads for the same reason.

The audio crews' vocal mic of choice is the AKG 535 condenser mic because it puts out the hottest levels and sounds great. The crew uses a variety of microphones, however, for the band. For the more mobile vocalists, there are several Cetec Vega Dynex 2 System wireless remote R42 diversity receivers coupled onto the back of the production mult splitter, with plenty of dipoles onstage for complete coverage. Quite often, though, vocalists just want a good old Shure SM57.

Showtime

After the final band rehearsal with cameras, the crew runs through a final soundcheck. There'll be a break before taping. Pete San Filipo and Mark Weber dress the cables and make final adjustments. Gradually appearing on the set, Posse players Mike Wolff, John B. Williams, Starr Parody, Peter Maunu and Chuck Morris take their places and start warming up.

In the control room, crew members take their positions. It's showtime. The show runs smoothly and, with all those hours of preparation,

Arsenio's band, The Posse

is the icing on the cake. After the wrap, roadies and crew people mill around the set. Chiate cheerily takes me aside. "It's like this," he says, "if you want to tape live acts, you have to go the extra mile to make the music happen. We're dealing with the MTV generation. They want sound, real sound. Before this show started, we submitted a budget to Paramount for what we needed to do it right. They thought we were crazy, but we stuck to our guns. Tom Bruehl, VP of video operations at Paramount, and his staff were extremely helpful in getting us state-of-the-art gear and technical support. Without him none of this would have ever happened."

Klimuck adds, "A lot of our success also has to do with our director, Sandi Fullerton. She used to direct *Rock Concert*, and she's really into music. No matter how many rehearsals we need or how much time we take, she's right behind us. A lot of directors won't do that."

It's evident that these people really like working together. The audio crew has been nominated once for an Emmy, and there is a tremendous spirit of cooperation.

"We're freelancers on this audio crew," says Klimuck. "We all do other projects, and that keeps this show fresh. We love to come here and work together, and Arsenio's a great guy. He loves music and he does whatever he can for us."

"Everyone works hard," comments Joe Hall, the man in charge of maintaining all the pro audio gear on Stage 29, "but we still have fun."

"Yeah," adds Bart. "If you can't have fun, go get another job."◔

The Academy Awards Broadcast

A Peek Behind The Scenes

BY AMY ZIFFER

"THE ACADEMY AWARDS SHOW is as much chaos as you can possibly throw at an individual from all directions, going out live to a viewing audience of one billion people. It's the greatest show on earth. The first time I did it, I was soaring for a week-and-a-half. When you nail the Academy Awards, you know you've done something."

That's the respect with which Lee DeCarlo, music mixer for the 1992 show and three previous ones, still regards the Academy Awards, even though he's a seasoned veteran. He spent five years as chief engineer of Record Plant, and after 23 years in this industry, you might think nothing would get him nervous, but you'd be wrong. The first year he did the Awards, he didn't even realize how rattled he was until, at the ten-seconds-to-air mark, he looked down at his hands and saw they were shaking violently.

DeCarlo is one of those rare people who meets with success in film, television and music, having been nominated for—and won—Emmys and Grammys for his work on the broadcast of the New York City Marathon and sessions with John Lennon, to name just a few.

He is responsible for all aspects of the Oscars' orchestral mix, generating feeds for the house mixer and production mixer, who generates the broadcast signal. DeCarlo's principal accomplice behind the console is "invaluable" ABC Television engineer and co-mixer Zoli Osaze, who has worked on 11 Academy Awards broadcasts, mixing many of them himself. Osaze also began his career in music, taking a job with ABC Records in 1973 and moving to the television division when the label was sold to MCA.

Preparation begins about a month before the awards, with DeCarlo watching and listening to last year's show. The "formal" preparation, however, begins with a meeting of all technical staff two weeks before the March 30 air date.

March 16, 10 a.m. Several hundred people crowd Stage 57 on the ABC Television lot in Hollywood, which happens to be the set of *America's Funniest Home Videos*. ("Appropriate," DeCarlo jokes.) These folks constitute the complete technical staff for the Academy Awards, from set designers to stage hands. The meeting comes to order. Director Jeff Margolis and producer Gil Cates have everyone introduce themselves; it's the first opportunity for some to meet the team. A short run-down of the script follows. It

Cindy Crawford and
paparazzi

takes about an hour. Roy Christopher, the set decorator, has a model of the set, complete with props. Before leaving, everyone is given a massive set of paperwork the size of a Gutenberg Bible; in fact, it will be their bible for the next two weeks.

DeCarlo works within a budget, and the money allocated has to cover everything from paying the orchestra to tape costs. Design FX has been contracted to provide remote truck services at the venue, the Dorothy Chandler Pavilion in downtown Los Angeles.

The orchestra will not only play at the Awards, but will also prerecord every number nominated in the Best Original Song category. The songs are performed in their entirety during the ceremony. Studio time for prerecords at Ocean Way in Hollywood was booked way back in November.

For this particular performance, the song "When You're Alone," from the movie *Hook*, is being prerecorded because it is sung by a six-year-old, and there is concern about her ability to perform it live on key. Another number, "Belle," from *Beauty and the Beast*, includes 16 separate solos by minor singers and players. None of them can use a handheld mic because they are also dancing, and 16 open lavalier mics running around onstage is out of the question. Only the leads, Paige O'Hara and Richard White, will sing live.

Even though these are the only two numbers for which prerecorded performances are planned, DeCarlo records and mixes four of the five, knowing anything can happen. The Academy Awards intimidates people. He's seen big names back out as the big day approaches.

"One year the director insisted everything would be live," he recalls, "but several performers wanted to go with prerecords. It was just luck that I had run a 2-track at the rehearsal sessions, and that's what went out on air. Since then, I've learned to prerecord everything."

The fifth song, Bryan Adams' "(Everything I Do) I Do It for You," is being handled by Greene/Crowe production mixer Paul Sandweiss with

> **"You have 2,500 people in the house and a billion people watching. When you weigh those two, the television audience wins. So you make little deals with the P.A. mixer: 'I'll give you more snare in the premix if you'll bring your overall down.'"** —Lee DeCarlo

Lee DeCarlo (left) and
Gary Ladinsky

supervision by Bob Clearmountain. It requires a completely different set and its own console.

March 24, 10:56 a.m. It's four minutes to downbeat on the day of the first read-through. Roughly 50 musicians, hundreds of instruments and several thousand feet of cable sprawl in seeming disarray across the whole of Ocean Way Studio One. The air conditioning must be working overtime to keep the studio from going supernova just from body heat alone. It's at moments like this that DeCarlo's unfailing good humor keeps the situation from degenerating into complete disorder. I approach him to ask where I should sit, expecting a harried brush-off. "Amy," he says instead, gesturing toward the harpist, "I'd like you to meet Dorothy."

Someone is stressed: In the control room a telltale blue bottle of milk of magnesia sits on the producer's desk, but nobody claims it. DeCarlo and Osaze have been there since 8:30; the two assistants, Steve Holroyd and Mark Guilbeault, since 9 a.m. Setup took the entire previous day.

A great deal of thought went into the arrangement of the players, because the sound from the prerecords must match the sound from the pit of the Dorothy Chandler Pavilion. This is especially critical because "Belle" segues directly into "Be Our Guest," also from *Beauty and the Beast*. The orchestra will have to pick up where the prerecord leaves off, and gross incongruities would be immediately obvious.

The read-through takes ten hours. Musical director and conductor Bill Conti and the orchestra look for bad notes and make sure the arrangements work. Lee's style is to concentrate as much on people as the music. As Angela Lansbury and Jerry Orbach arrive, he tells an assistant, "If you ever see a star coming in, run out to meet them and make them feel important." He makes sure they have a cup of coffee, and that everyone is introduced, because he knows the talent is the *raison d'être* for the show. Their comfort will translate into a better performance and a better time for all.

March 25-26: Prerecords and mixing.

The prerecords go down to analog 24-track running at 15 ips, +3dB, non-Dolby. It is mixed down to a 1/4-inch 2-track and 1/2-inch 4-track, also running at 15 ips, +3 dB. "You don't want to get fancy when it comes to television," DeCarlo says. "No elevated levels beyond the norm, nothing unusual."

The 2-track contains two versions, one with no vocals and one with all vocals. It's primarily for rehearsal purposes. The 4-track will go out for broadcast from the Greene/Crowe truck. In addition to a left and right stereo mix of the orchestra, it contains the lead and background vocals, each on their own track. The lead vocal will be omitted from playback during broadcast because the two leads sing live, but they could be used as a backup in an emergency.

While mixdown is being done at Ocean Way, Design FX crew members Mark Eshelman and Bruce Maddox are at Dorothy Chandler setting up the pit. Lee has graphed out the musician's positions to scale on a pit plan, calculating the number of square feet allocated to each one. Despite holding half as many people in the house, the Dorothy Chandler orchestra pit is downright spacious compared to the Shrine Auditorium, where the show has been held in previous years.

Players are positioned so that mic leakage helps, rather than hinders, the overall sound, an important consideration since most of the mics are condensers. For example, violin or viola mics might pick up enough of the drums to eliminate the need for overheads.

Despite the need to match the live sound to the prerecords, the mic lists for the Ocean Way sessions and the pit are not identical. "It would hurt you if they were identical," DeCarlo insists. "Some mics are just much better in a studio situation." Ambience is a far more overriding factor than whether the floor tom is miked with a U87 or a 452. The goal is to make the mix on tape and the mix in the venue as good as possible while still being compatible.

Terry Stark (left) and Jack Crymes aboard the Design FX truck

No sooner are the prerecords mixed than it's off to the venue for a 7 p.m. soundcheck. For the next two days, DeCarlo and Osaze are on-site from 8 a.m. to midnight—rehearsing, working out bugs and fine-tuning the sound.

March 30, 1:36 p.m. Full dress rehearsal, with stand-in presenters and dancers. Crowds of gawkers are jostling for position near the arrivals area. It's only with the help of Terry Stark, Design FX's remote recording division director, that I pass muster and am credentialed. The sound truck is next to Paul Newman's and Elizabeth Taylor's trailers, which causes me to speculate on the street value of the backstage pass I'm wearing. DeCarlo says $500, easy.

For the last four days, DeCarlo and Osaze have been supplementing the script with notes of their own, describing in plain terms what will happen and when. They note the type of underscoring, tympani rolls, brass hits and so forth, with some dialog lines for guidance. These notes are computer-output and inserted in the three-ring bible with the scripted ones. During rehearsal and again during the show, Osaze calls out these notes to DeCarlo. With roughly 240 different pieces of music, it's too much for him to memorize. And at this point, production or direction might still be dropping things from the script.

"The show is so fast, it's just crazy," DeCarlo says, shaking his head. "You never get to rehearse the whole thing. Even the dress rehearsal is a stop-and-go kind of thing."

Television monitors provide three views of the inside of the venue. The largest is dedicated to broadcast signal. A smaller one gives DeCarlo a continuous wide-angle view of the stage, so he can see artists coming on or going off. And a third one is always fixed on Bill Conti.

In stark contrast to the limited visual contact, DeCarlo is bombarded with voices coming out of P.L. (Push and Listen) boxes lined up on top of the patch bay, as well as a pair of Anchor speakers under the console, to which he must be attuned even while mixing. One of the Anchors is dedicated to a mic next to Conti; it's on at all times and is for private communication. (The P.L. boxes are broadcast devices, and anyone with a receiver can tune in.) The other Anchor is a feed from the Greene/Crowe truck with all the audio elements *except* the orchestra, which acts as his cue to the action inside.

On one or another channel of five different P.L. boxes, DeCarlo can talk or listen to the following: two Design FX staff members in the pit; the director and assistant director; conductor Conti; the producer; the stage managers; production mixer Paul Sandweiss; the P.A. mixer, Patrick Baltzell; and the monitor mixer, Mike Abbott.

2:30 p.m. There's a break, and I get a tour of the pit from Osaze.

The pit is 47 feet wide and 19 feet deep at the center, tapering to 15 feet at either end. At the lowest point, there is seven feet of headroom. Because not every musician has a direct line of sight to the conductor, pairs of video monitors are scattered about, positioned to give everyone a view of both Conti and the broadcast signal. Conti himself has a trio of monitors with the same feeds DeCarlo has in the truck. There is barely enough room for two people to pass between the rows of chairs.

With 45 open microphones in a space this small, "the sound almost mixes itself," according to Osaze. "It's not true stereo; we don't have the luxury of using a couple of overheads and having individual mics flesh things out. Everything must be miked individually, and we have to rely a lot on the foldback and P.A. mixers not to overdrive their systems." If they do, the sound will be picked up by the mics in the pit and will muddy the music mix or create feedback loops. This is especially critical because most of the mics are condensers.

DeCarlo calls the Dorothy Chandler Pavilion, with its 2,500 seats and three balconies, a "good sounding house," a "polite"

Mixing the Sound at the Academy Awards

The Design FX truck has a 44-input API console with Penn Stevens input modules and 550 EQs. Both the big monitors and the close-fields are by KRK. All the mics on the orchestra (roughly 45 in all) are fed into the truck and mixed by Lee DeCarlo down to two channels. He sends the P.A. mixer the following stereo pairs: brass, rhythm, woods, strings, vocals and an overall mix.

The overall mix is also sent to the Greene/Crowe broadcast truck where it's combined with the podium mic signal, live applause picked up in the house, and a supplemental applause and laugh track. The prerecords originate here, as well.

Audio is integrated with video and most graphics on site, then sent to the ABC Television facility in Hollywood by Pacific Bell, using either microwave transmission or coaxial cable. There, the signal is "integrated," i.e., commercials are added. ABC uplinks to an AT&T Telstar 301 satellite on which it owns transponders. The signal is then backhauled to ABC New York, where it goes through their normal network distribution channels (involving another uplink to a second Telstar 301 for downlink by ABC's affiliates).

DeCarlo's cue mix arrangement is somewhat of a Rube Goldberg affair. He doesn't want the mix minus orchestra running into the console and then into the cue bus, because it opens the door to blunders and the danger of crosstalk. Instead, it's running through an 1176, and the music mix is running through another. The limiters' two output knobs, acting as attenuators, give him complete control over both balance and overall volume. The cue system is switched to mono mode.

"If you have a lot of transients," DeCarlo says, "the limiters will pump. They are in the signal chain, and there's nothing I can do about it. So the goal is to get them engaged and make them stay where they are." He puts a pair of Pultec EQP-1 equalizers across the stereo mix and boosts around 30 Hz and 12 kHz. Since the microwave transmission lines are relatively narrow band, very little of those emphasized frequencies ever make it to TV. "The only thing it does is make the limiters work. Then within that limiting, I fine-tune my mix." He also uses the EQP-1s to brighten the midrange as needed when the wash of applause dulls the apparent sound of the music mix.

room. "You don't need a lot of sound reinforcement," he says. "Strings and woodwinds need the most help. The drums practically carry themselves; the P.A. mixer may have to reach for them just a little."

There has to be some compromise to the house sound to enable the broadcast quality to be tops. "You have 2,500 people in the house," DeCarlo says, "and a billion people watching. When you weigh those two, the television audience wins. So you make little deals with the P.A. mixer: 'I'll give you more snare in the premix if you'll bring your overall down.'"

3:45 p.m. With the rehearsal over, DeCarlo is not happy. "Bad rehearsal, good show," he says to anyone who asks how things are going. While everyone else goes off to find food, DeCarlo won't be eating; one year he got food poisoning and had to work throwing up into a wastebasket. The next two hours are a waiting game. Just before 5:30, Mark Eshelman and Design FX's maintenance technician Jack Crymes do a last check of the mics. Everything is working. About the same time, almost everyone who's been slouching around the truck all afternoon in jeans and T-shirts disappears, only to return clad in tuxedos. DeCarlo has apparently changed, too; then I see he's still wearing leather pants.

"No matter how much preparation we do," he sighs, "after the musicians come back from dinner, everything is different. And once they start, we have only 8 minutes and 59 seconds—the length of the overture—to fix it."

During the last 20 minutes, the air in the truck takes on a definite charge. At 5:51, Conti raises his baton, and DeCarlo turns and says with a completely straight face, "I've just forgotten the entire show." He lets out a primal scream and the orchestra begins. Almost immediately, there is a sound of rustling fabric and whispering. DeCarlo grabs a P.L. box and asks someone in the pit to remind the singers that their every movement can be heard through their open mic. Things settle down, and DeCarlo slowly begins dancing in his seat. By air time, he's already in a groove.

The show is much funnier behind the scenes than viewers ever see. Minor mistakes and surprises happen constantly, and every time one does, the P.L. boxes explode with screaming voices. Everyone gasps, "What's he doing?" when Best Supporting Actor winner Jack Palance unexpectedly moves off mic and commences doing push-ups. When 100-year-old producing legend Hal Roach thanks the Academy from his seat and there is no mic to pick him up, everyone cheers Billy Crystal's clever save. Conti conducts furiously even during the prerecords, just in case someone turns a camera on him.

Diplomacy is invaluable during rehearsal, but there's rarely time for it during the show. Everyone has to be able to take their lumps and correct the problem *fast*. "The only people with thin skins are those who don't know what they're doing," DeCarlo says. "Everyone else knows that you mess up all day long. You're not supposed to, of course, but if you do, you have to be smart enough to keep moving and not panic."

But nothing happens this year to cause panic. Except for a small problem with a pumping limiter down the line near the start of the show, it's relatively uneventful. The hours fly by. Occasionally DeCarlo checks the time; he's got five dollars in the orchestra pool riding on the length of the show.

> The show is much funnier behind the scenes than viewers ever see. Minor mistakes and surprises happen constantly, and every time one does, the P.L. boxes explode with screaming voices.

Dances with Oscars: Stagehands prepare for the ceremony.

By the midway point, it's obvious that everything's under control and will likely stay that way.

10:33 p.m. Show's over. As Academy members filter out the front doors of the Pavilion toward a reception tent pitched outdoors where dinner awaits, DeCarlo makes his way to the pit. The Design FX staff is already starting to break down.

> "It's the greatest show on earth. The first time I did it, I was soaring for a week-and-a-half. When you nail the Academy Awards, you know you've done something." —Lee DeCarlo

"Time to bond with the orchestra," he explains. "I really do love them. I fawn over them. I've been accepted by them in a relatively short time—four years—and the only reason is because I care about them. They would never screw me, and I would never screw them."

In many ways, that seems to be the key to the whole thing: a little give and take, a little consideration for the next guy, and the teamwork necessary to pull off such a demanding production will happen.

DeCarlo is elated, and with good reason. He's pulled it off again. He's calmer than he was that first year, but mixing the music for the Academy Awards is still obviously the thrill of a lifetime. ⊙

CD Production Music And Sound Effects Libraries

I**T'S NO SECRET** that today's production music and sound effects libraries are better than ever. Besides the well-known advantages of compact discs—improved sound quality, 60- to 70-minute storage capacity and relative imperviousness to scratches and other physical damage—the CD medium offers quick cueing and the ability to rapidly audition different selections, two obvious advantages in a quick-paced production environment.

Production Music Libraries

Music libraries offer an almost overwhelming diversity of available material: classical, folk, country, jazz, rock, fusion, rap, dance, religious, new age, ethnic, children's, period pieces, traditional, patriotic, historical, electronic and everybody's all-purpose favorite, middle-of-the-road.

Licensing contracts and rates can take a variety of forms. Typically, a buyout agreement allows the unlimited use of music for a one-time charge. An "annual blanket" offers unlimited library use for a yearly payment. A "per-production" rate allows the unlimited use of a particular library or selection in a single production for a set fee, which depends on the audience market size/type, distribution medium and the project's total length. A "theme rate" covers the use of a particular selection on several projects, especially in jingles, television ads and radio spots. "Needle-drop" refers to the use of a partial or entire music selection in a single segment of a production. Therefore, if the same theme is used in two different parts of a film, then two needle-drop charges would apply.

A User's Guide

BY GEORGE PETERSEN

With an extremely wide range of possible applications and audience markets for production music, an equally wide range of charges can apply. For example, a needle-drop fee for a bed used on a local radio spot may be as low as $25; however, if that same piece of music is spotlighted in a network television program or theatrical film release, the license fee would undoubtedly be much higher. Libraries offering music on a licensed basis generally distribute music CDs for a nominal charge (usually $10 to $15 per disc—*not* including usage fees) or provide a collection of CDs as part of a blanket license. As an alternative, some companies will loan discs on an "approval" basis, allowing the producer to audition disc(s) before committing to a license. The latter is commonly applied to specialty CDs such as historical, classical, international or ethnic music when there is only an occasional need for such material.

You'll have to do some research to find a library whose music and use arrangements best fit your needs. Buyout, per-use and blanket licenses all afford different advantages and disadvantages depending on your particular situation, and it's best to weigh all the facts before you decide. In some instances it may be preferable to have a little of both worlds by using a buyout or long-term license library for everyday "bread-and-butter" production chores and adding occasional needle-drop cuts for variety. Of course, there's no law that says you can't use two or more different libraries. Your limits should be dictated by your budget and/or production needs.

Some decisions are simple: For example, a hot set of 30- and 60-second jingle beds is an inappropriate choice for the dramatic film producer. The subjective evaluation of the quality of a library's offerings is a more difficult ques-

tion—after all, no one knows your musical needs better than you. Fortunately, all the companies listed in this report will provide demos upon request.

Sound Effects

Like production music libraries, sound effects collections have improved immeasurably over the past five years. The emergence of portable DAT recorders has increased the quality of field recordings. And recently, more film studios and large production houses have released their collections on CD for commercial sale. Today there are dozens of sound effects libraries—literally hundreds of discs—offered by various companies serving the pro audio market.

With so many sound effects CDs available, the logistics of dealing with the sheer numbers of discs and tracks can be problematic. Many companies now provide some sort of track search/cross-reference database program with the libraries, either as an option or in addition to the printed catalog/index that comes with the library.

Third-party suppliers such as Gefen Systems (Woodland Hills, Calif.) and Leonardo Software of Los Angeles offer database software that can cross-reference, control and retrieve discs from several libraries of different companies, working with the Sony CDK-006, a CD "jukebox" player with the capacity to handle up to 60 discs. Gefen also offers the "SFX Log," a directory in book form that lists and cross-references the sound effects available from most major libraries.

The recent popularity of CD sound effects libraries probably stems from that same availability of affordable, yet high-quality, recording gear that spawned the project studio over the past decade. Equipped with a modest recording setup, some MIDI gear and a music and sound effects library or two, it is possible to do an impressive (i.e., profitable) amount of film/video scoring, sweetening or radio production work, even within the confines of the smallest control room.

Another factor in the popularity of CD effects is the ease with which they can be manipulated in the digital domain. After loading sounds into a sampler or disk-based editing system, effects can be cut, spliced, extended, looped, pitch shifted, reversed or all of the above. Later, it is a relatively simple matter to fly these new effects into a mix synched to SMPTE time code or triggered by a MIDI sequencer. In fact, a sampler or workstation system is also handy when you want to use two effects from the same disc (e.g., meadow ambience and cows mooing) during a live mix.

A recent trend is the advent of highly specialized mini-libraries—such as the Sound Ideas "Wheels" (automotive sounds) set, Dorsey's "The Works" (2,800 mechanical and industrial sounds) or the Prosonus Foley Disc (footsteps)—that can be added as an adjunct to a general sound effects collection.

Additionally, many companies now offer discs from their libraries on an a la carte basis. In such a case, you can buy only what you need, whether it's weather, household, transportation, animals or other sounds.

Responding to market requests, many companies now offer longer effects for background ambience. While somewhat outside the realm of this article, an increasing number of companies are releasing sound effects in the CD-ROM format, ready for loading into digital samplers of all sorts.

Most sound effects CDs tend to fall within the $30 to $60 per disc price range. While this cost may seem somewhat steep, a decent sound effects library can be had for about the cost of a quality studio microphone. Of course, when you consider the time required to go out and record a bunch of crazed bull elephants, perhaps the price isn't so bad after all.

The following section includes more than 45 firms that have production music and/or sound effects collections on CD, ranging from small "boutique" suppliers to large operations with hundreds of discs from several libraries.

Production Music And Sound Effects Libraries

The bracketed data under each company's name indicates the type of products offered: "SFX" refers to sound effects CDs; "Buyout PM" refers to production music available on a one-time purchase; and "Signatory PM" indicates production music licensed on needle-drop, per-use, per-production or annual blanket arrangements.

AirCraft Music Library
[SFX, Signatory PM]
77 N. Washington St.
Boston, MA 02114
(617) 367-4962, (800) 343-2514

Airforce Broadcast Services
[Signatory PM]
216 Carlton St., Suite 300
Toronto, ON, M5A 2L1 Canada
(416) 961-2541

Associated Production Music
[SFX, Signatory PM]
6255 Sunset Blvd., Suite 820
Hollywood, CA 90028
(213) 461-3211, (800) 543-4276

Audio Action
[SFX, Signatory PM]
4444 Lakeside Dr., Suite 340
Burbank, CA 91510
(818) 845-8020, (800) 533-1293

Audio Concepts
[Buyout PM]
1653 Merriman Rd.
Akron, OH 44313
(216) 867-4448, (800) 788-1233

Audisee
[SFX, Signatory PM]
621 East Pike
Seattle, WA 98122
(206) 323-6476

Bainbridge Entertainment Company
[SFX]
Box 8248
Van Nuys, CA 91409
(213) 476-0631

Bonardi & Associates
[SFX]
20 Sunnyside Ave. #A108
Mill Valley, CA 94941
(415) 435-2759

Brown Bag Productions
[Signatory PM]
4134 S. Eudora St.
Englewood, CO 80110
(303) 756-9949

Capitol Production Music
[Signatory PM]
6922 Hollywood Blvd., Suite 718
Hollywood, CA 90028
(213) 461-2701, (800) 421-4163

CBS Sound Effects Library
[SFX]
CBS Special Products
51 W. 52nd St.
New York, NY 10106
Also distributed by Mix Bookshelf:
(800) 233-9604, (510) 653-3307

Century 21 Programming
[SFX, Signatory PM]
14444 West Beltwood Pkwy.
Dallas, TX 75244
(214) 934-2121, (800) 937-2100

Comprehensive Video Supply
[SFX, Buyout PM]
148 Veterans Dr.
Northvale, NJ 07647
(201) 767-7990

Creative Support Services
[SFX, Buyout PM]
1950 Riverside Dr.
Los Angeles, CA 90039
(213) 666-7968, (800) HOT-MUSIC

De Wolfe Music Library
[SFX, Signatory PM]
25 West 45th St.
New York, NY 10036
(212) 382-0220, (800) 221-6713

Dorsey Productions
[SFX]
2453 E. Virginia Ave.
Anaheim, CA 92806
(714) 535-3344, (800) 735-4366

Firstcom/Music House
[SFX, Signatory PM]
13747 Monfort Dr., Suite 220
Dallas, TX 75240
(214) 934-2222, (800) 858-8880

Gefen Systems
[SFX, Buyout PM]
6261 Variel Ave., Suite C
Woodland Hills, CA 91367
(818) 884-6294, (800) 545-6900

Hanna-Barbera Sound Effects Library
[SFX]
Distributed by Interlock Music Dept.
Box 4542
Chatsworth, CA 91311
(213) 461-2500

The Hollywood Edge
[SFX]
7060 Hollywood Blvd., Suite 1120
Hollywood, CA 90028
(213) 466-6723, (800) 292-3755

Hollywood Film Music Library
[Signatory PM]
11684 Ventura Blvd., Suite 850
Studio City, CA 91604
(818) 985-9997

James & Aster
[SFX, Signatory PM]
115 East 23rd St.
New York, NY 10010
(212) 982-0300, (800) 572-2236

Killer Tracks
[SFX, Signatory PM]
6534 Sunset Blvd.
Hollywood, CA 90028
(213) 957-4455, (800) 877-0078

Manhattan Production Music
[SFX, Signatory PM]
311 W. 43rd St., Suite 702
New York, NY 10036
(212) 333-5766, (800) 227-1954

Metro Music
[Signatory PM]
645 West End Ave.
New York, NY 10025
(212) 799-7600

MusiCrafters
[Buyout PM]
Box 595
Montgomeryville, PA 18936
(215) 368-8863

Musikos Inc.
[SFX, Buyout PM]
2121 Commonwealth Ave.,
Suite 102
Charlotte, NC 28205
(704) 333-6900, (800) 627-1012

Network Music
[SFX, Signatory PM]
110 Via Frontera
San Diego, CA 92127
(619) 451-6400, (800) 854-2075

NFL Films Music Library
[Signatory PM]
330 Fellowship Rd.
Mt. Laurel, NJ 08054
(609) 778-1600

O'Connor Creative
[SFX]
Box 5432
Playa Del Rey, CA 90296
(213) 827-2527

Omnimusic
[SFX, Signatory PM]
52 Main St.
Port Washington, NY 11050
(516) 883-0121, (800) 828-OMNI

Philadelphia Music Works
[SFX, Buyout PM]
Box 947
Bryn Mawr, PA 19010
(215) 825-5656, (800) 368-0033

Producers Sound Effects Library
[SFX]
8033 Sunset Blvd. #289
Hollywood, CA 90046
(818) 707-EFXS, (800) 826-3397

Production Garden
[SFX, Buyout PM]
2411 NE Loop 410, Suite 132
San Antonio, TX 78217
(512) 599-9439, (800) 247-5317

Promusic
[SFX, Signatory PM]
6555 NW Ninth Ave. #303
Ft. Lauderdale, FL 33309
(305) 776-2070

Prosonus
[SFX, Buyout PM]
11126 Weddington St.
North Hollywood, CA 91601
(818) 766-5221, (800) 999-6191

QCCS Productions
[Buyout PM]
1350 Chambers
Eugene, OR 97402
(503) 345-0212

River City Sound
[Buyout PM]
Box 750786
Memphis, TN 38175-0786
(901) 274-7277, (800) 755-8729

Signature Music
[SFX, Buyout PM]
Box 98
Buchanan, MI 49107
(616) 695-3068, (800) 888-7151

Soper Sound Library
[Buyout PM]
Box 498
Palo Alto, CA 94301
(415) 321-4022, (800) 227-9980

Sound Ideas
[SFX, Signatory PM]
105 W. Beaver Creek Rd. #4
Richmond Hill, ON,
L4B-1C6 Canada
(416) 886-5000, (800) 387-3030

Sounds Interesting Productions
[Buyout & Signatory PM]
922 Massachusetts Ave. #12
Cambridge, MA 02139
(617) 876-1646

Southern Library of Recorded Music
[Signatory PM]
6777 Hollywood Blvd. #209
Hollywood, CA 90028
(213) 469-9910

Techsonics
[Signatory PM]
709 Shadowfield Ct.
Chesapeake, VA 23320
(804) 547-4000

TRF Production Music
[SFX, Signatory PM]
1619 Broadway
New York, NY 10019
(212) 265-8090, (800) 899-MUSIC

27th Dimension Inc.
[SFX, Buyout PM]
Box 1149
Okeechobee, FL 34973-1149
(813) 763-4107, (800) 634-0091

Valentino Inc.
[SFX, Signatory PM]
151 W. 46th St.
New York, NY 10036
(212) 869-5210, (800) 223-6278

Zedz Music
[Buyout PM]
49 Hanover St.
Malden, MA 02148
(617) 324-1989

ZM Squared
[SFX, Buyout PM]
Box 2030
Cinnaminson, NJ 08077
(609) 786-0612

Glossary

A-B Roll: Reels consisting of camera-original film and opaque leader, spliced together and ready for printing at the lab. Optical effects such as fades and dissolves can be made by providing a cue sheet with exposure control instructions to the printer for each roll at corresponding footage markers.

ADR: Automatic Dialog Replacement. Also known as "looping." A process of re-recording dialog in the studio in synchronization with the picture. Actors watch the picture in "loops," then synchronize lip movements to picture in order to get a clean dialog track.

Address Track: A control/timing track on the edge of videotape (1-inch C and 3/4-inch formats) that contains control data for quick and accurate location of program material; recorded at the same time as picture.

Ambient Sound: Sounds such as reverberation, noise and atmosphere that form a background to the main sound taking place at any given moment. The lack of ambient sound is noticeable because the ear expects it.

Analog Recording: A means of recording audio or video whereby the recorded signal is a physical representation of the waveform of the original signal.

Anti-Aliasing: Filtering of erroneous frequencies that are created during the analog-to-digital conversion process.

Beat: A periodic variation of amplitude resulting from the addition of two slightly different frequencies.

Bed: Background music used underneath a narrator or foreground dialog. Primarily applied to commercial radio or television spots. Also called "basic tracks."

Blocking: Plotting actor, camera and mic placement and movement in a production.

Burn-in Time Code: A videotape in which a "window" displaying the time code count on the tape is superimposed over part of the picture. Eliminates the need to watch a time code reader. Accurate in still frame.

Bus: A mixing network that combines the output of two or more channels. A recording console may contain many buses (mix bus, monitor bus, channel bus, ground bus, etc.).

CD: Compact Disc. A digitally encoded disc, 4.7 inches in diameter, capable of containing more than one hour of music at a sampling frequency of 44.1 kHz. Data is read by a laser beam.

Click Track: A prerecorded track of electronic metronomic clicks used to ensure proper timing of music to be recorded. Essential in music scoring sessions. Typically recorded on one track of a multitrack.

Compander: A combination of the words compressor and expander. Refers to a device that compresses an input signal and expands the output signal in order to reduce noise.

Compression: The reduction of a signal's output level in relation to its input level in order to reduce dynamic range.

Condenser Microphone: Developed at Bell Labs and introduced commercially in 1931. The simplest type of microphone in which the capacitance (electrical charge) is varied by sound, causing movement in one plate (diaphragm) in relation to a fixed backplate. Also known as capacitor microphone or pressure microphone.

Control Track: A series of pulses recorded automatically on a videotape to resolve the playback speed by controlling and synchronizing the video frames.

Crossfade: The fading in of one sound source as another fades out. At some point the sounds cross at an equal volume.

Crosstalk: Also known as "bleeding." Any unwanted leakage of one audio signal into another, usually occurring between adjacent tracks. Time code signals can also crosstalk into audio tracks.

Cue List: Also called "cue sheet." A list of the footages and frames, beginning with 0:00, at which specific shots begin and end. Used by the re-recording mixer who needs to know which sounds or music must be played as the final mix proceeds. See also Edit Decision List.

Cutter: Slang term for a sound editor.

Cycles: Short for "cycles-per-second." Also known as Hertz, the unit for measuring frequency.

Dailies: Also known as "rushes." The first print from the lab of the film shot on the previous day, usually with the synchronous sound transferred to magnetic film for "double system" projection. Directors and producers view dailies regularly to chart the progress of a production.

DAT: Digital Audio Tape. Two-channel digital audio. Has become increasingly common as a professional master reference and for use in field recording.

DAW: Digital Audio Workstation. A computer-based recording/editing machine for manipulating sounds.

Dialog Track: The edited track on magnetic film containing the dialog portion of a film's sound. Sometimes there may be a separate track for each actor in a scene. Separate dialog tracks may be "mixed down" into a single track.

Digital Recording: A method of recording in which samples of the original analog signal are encoded on tape or disk as binary information for storage or processing. The signal can then be copied repeatedly with no degradation.

Dolby SR: Spectral Recording. An encoding/decoding noise reduction system developed by Dolby Laboratories and used increasingly in film sound.

Double-System Sound: Sound and picture on separate transports (e.g., film and Nagra, film and mag dubber, videotape and audio tape).

Drop-In: The process of inserting recorded audio by playing up to a chosen point and switching from playback to record mode.

Drop Frame: American system of time code generation that adjusts the generated data every minute to compensate for the speed of the NTSC television system running at 29.97 frames per second.

Dub: To make a taped copy of any program source—record, CD, tape. Also, the copy itself. Sometimes used to refer to the ADR process.

Dub Stage: Term used in California but not on the East Coast to refer to the room where the final audio mix is made for a program or film. Also known as mix stage.

Dynamic Range: The range between the quietest and loudest sounds that a sound source can produce without distortion.

EBU: European Broadcast Union. Identifies a 25 FPS time code standard.

Edit Decision List (EDL): The list of SMPTE codes—in footage and frames, and including instructions for fades, dissolves and other special effects—corresponding to all the segments that the editor of a videotape production has decided to use in the final cut. Sometimes handwritten, but usually computer-generated.

Edit Master: Video industry term for the tape containing the finished (edited) program.

Edit Points: Also known as "edit in" and "edit out." The beginning and end points of an edit when a video program or soundtrack is being assembled.

Envelope: The shape of the graph as amplitude is plotted against time. A sound's envelope includes its attack, decay, sustain and release (ADSR).

EQ: Short for equalization. The boosting or decreasing of the intensity of low, middle and high frequencies in order to change the sound of program material.

F1: A reference to the (now discontinued) Sony PCM-F1 digital recording system, which uses an EIAJ-format 16-bit Pulse Code Modulation processor to convert audio into a digital form that can be stored on videotape.

Feet/Frames: Footage numbers for film, separated by a colon. For example, 101:16 indicates a point 101 feet and 16 frames into the film. There are 16 frames per foot of 35mm film; 40 frames per foot of 16mm film.

Field Rate: Frequency rate at which video fields occur: 59.94 Hz in NTSC, 50 Hz in PAL European format.

Flatbed: A modern film or sound editing system where reels are laid horizontally on "plates" on a mechanized table with sound and picture heads. Manufactured by companies such as KEM, Moviola and Steenbeck.

Foley: Creating sound effects by watching picture and mimicking the action, often with props that do not exactly match the action. On a Foley stage, Foley artists, also known as Foley "walkers," make use of a variety of objects and/or surfaces to elicit realistic sound effects that can't be gathered by other means. Most common in recording footsteps, hence the term "walkers."

Frame: A single photographic image on film; one complete screen on videotape.

Frame Rate: Frequency at which video frames occur: 29.97 Hz in NTSC, 25 Hz in PAL European format.

Frequency: The number of times per second that a sound source vibrates, expressed in Hertz (Hz).

Full-Coat: Magnetic film coated with oxide across its entire width; available in 16mm and 35mm formats.

Full-Stripe: Magnetic film with oxide coating in just the area where the recording takes place, allowing the transparent material to be written on.

Gain: The ratio of the signal level at the output of an audio device to the signal level at its input. Expressed in decibels (dB).

Gigabyte (GB): A unit for measuring computer memory capacity, equivalent to 1,000 megabytes (MB).

Hard Disk: A data storage and retrieval device consisting of a disk drive and one or more permanently installed disks. Increasingly common for storing sound effects and archiving for future use. The big advantage is random access.

Highpass Filters: A filter that attenuates frequencies below a specified frequency and allows those above that point to pass.

House Sync: An internal timing reference used to synchronize all transports within a facility.

Hertz (Hz): Unit for measuring frequency of a signal; formerly called "cycles per second."

Insert Editing: Used in videotape or digital audio editing to describe the process of replacing a segment located between two specific and previously dubbed segments. The editor usually refers to SMPTE time code numbers or "addresses."

Interlock: A term that generically refers to two or more machines running in sychronization; often shortened to "locked."

Jam Sync: A process of locking a time code generator to an existing coded tape in order to extend or replace the code, used when code is of poor quality.

Lavalier Mic: A small microphone that can be easily hidden on a piece of clothing so as not to be seen by the camera.

Layback: Transfer of the finished audio mix back onto the video edit master.

Layoff: Transfer of audio and time code from the video edit master to an audio tape.

Layover: Transfer of audio onto multitrack tape or hard disk. Also referred to as "layup."

Lip Sync: Synchronization of picture and sound that is accurate to the point that the actor's lip movements and words appear simultaneously to the viewer: The goal of the ADR process and of music videos. Even a one-frame difference is noticeable.

Longitudinal Time Code: See SMPTE Time Code.

Looping: See Automatic Dialog Replacement.

Lowpass Filter: A filter that attenuates frequencies above a specified frequency and allows those below that point to pass.

L-C-R-S: Left, Center, Right, Surround. The four playback channels used in 35mm motion pictures, now available on home hi-fi systems. L, C and R speakers are located behind the screen. The S channel surrounds the audience and may be mono or encoded stereo.

M & E: Music & Effects soundtrack. A final film or television mix that leaves off the dialog track, then is sent overseas for foreign language dubs of dialog in specific countries.

Mag: Shorthand for magnetic film. Sprocketed film that contains only sound—no picture.

MB: The acronym for megabytes, a measure of computer storage capability; the equivalent of 1,000 bytes.

MIDI: Musical Instrument Digital Interface. A machine protocol that allows synthesizers, computers, drum machines and other processors to communicate with and/or control one another.

Moviola: Trade name (used generically) for an upright film editing machine common in the U.S.; contains a mono speaker.

Multichannel: In film, used to refer to a final mix that includes more than stereo information; i.e., LCRS or six-channel surround formats.

Multitrack: An audio tape recorder capable of handling more than two tracks of information separately.

NTSC: National Television Standards Committee. The organization that sets the American broadcast and videotape format standards for the FCC. Color television is set at 525 lines per frame, 29.97 frames per second.

Offline: The videotape editing process whereby the final edit list is compiled, usually in a more inexpensive edit room, in preparation for the on-line edit. Typically takes place on a 3/4-inch video deck.

Online: The videotape editing process that creates the final video edit master, including effects, from the offline edit list. Usually takes place on a 1-inch video deck.

Optical Recording: Sound recording on film. The photographically printed soundtrack is known as the optical track.

PAL: Phase Alternating Line. The European color television standard that specifies a 25Hz frame rate and 625 lines per frame.

Pilot Tone: A sine wave signal, recorded by Nagra field audio recorders at a known frequency, used to resolve the tape speed on playback to retain sync with film camera footage.

Post-Production: The period in a project's development that takes place after the picture is delivered, or "after the production." Can apply to video/film editing or refer to audio post-production.

Production Sound: Recording and/or mixing sound on location during the film or video shoot. Typically recorded to an analog Nagra reel-to-reel machine, though DAT recorders made significant inroads in the early 1990s.

Re-recording: The process of mixing all edited music, effects and dialog tracks of a film or video production to mono, stereo, multichannel or whatever audio format is desired for the final print master.

Resolving: The process of regulating tape speed by comparing a reference signal on the tape with an external reference and adjusting the speed so that they match.

Room Tone: The "noise" of a room, set or location where dialog is recorded for the production shoot. Used by film and dialog editors as a "bed" to form a continuous tone through a particular scene. Not to be confused with ambience, which can be sound effects and/or reverberation added when the dialog is mixed.

Score: The original-music composition for a motion picture or television production, recorded after the picture has been edited.

Scrub: Moving a piece of tape or magnetic film back and forth over the sound head to locate a specific cue or word.

Scrub Wheel: A mechanical control for scrubbing film or magnetic tape.

Sequencer: The hardware- or software-based brain of a MIDI studio. It receives, stores and plays back MIDI information in a desired sequence. Useful in scoring applications.

Shotgun Mic: A highly directional microphone with a long, tubular body; used by the production sound mixer on location or on the set for film and television productions.

Single-Stripe: Magnetic film that contains a single audio track, which is coated with oxide.

Single System: A method of recording sound and picture on the same medium, most typically used in news gathering and lower-budget industrial/educational productions. (See also Double System.)

Slave: An audio tape or videotape transport, projector or mag film dubber whose movements follow the movement of a single master transport. Accomplished electronically by using SMPTE time code numbers or mechanically by motor linkage of sprocketed machines.

SMPTE Time Code: Also known as Longitudinal Time Code. A high-frequency signal that allows the accurate "locking" of film audio and video equipment. Locator information is displayed as numbers. SMPTE stands for The Society of Motion Picture and Television Engineers.

Sound Effect: A recorded or electronically produced sound that matches the visual action taking place onscreen.

Soundtrack: Generically refers to the music contained in a film, though it literally means the entire audio portion of a film, video or television production, including effects and dialog. Also refers to the physical space on film that contains the audio information.

Splice: The joint made between two pieces of tape or film in the editing process.

Spotting: Used in scoring to identify the specific scenes where music cues will take place, including information on length and style. The composer will often spot a film, then re-spot it with director's feedback.

Stripe: (v.) To record time code on a blank audio tape or videotape.

Surround Sound: Sound that is reproduced through speakers above or behind the audience.

Sweeten/Sweetening: Enhancing the sound of a recording or a particular sound effect with equalization or some other signal processing device. Can be done during editing or mixing.

Telecine: A machine that transfers film to a video signal for broadcast or storage on videotape. Also generically refers to the process of film-to-tape transfers.

Time Code: See SMPTE Time Code.

Underscore: Music that provides emotional or atmospheric background to the primary dialog or narration onscreen.

Varispeed: Increasing or decreasing tape speed to match the musical pitch of a tape playback to the tuning of a sound source being over-dubbed.

VITC: Vertical Interval Time Code. A time code signal that is written in the vertical interval by the rotating video heads, allowing it to be read when the tape is not moving. Requires special equipment to read and write.

Voice-over: Narration or non-synchronous dialog taking place over the action onscreen.

Walla: Background ambience or noises added to create the illusion of sound taking place outside of the main action in a picture (e.g., street and traffic noise creating an urban atmosphere).

Wild Track: Audio elements that are not recorded synchronously with the picture.

Workprint: Copies of the original film or video used as a reference during the sound and/or picture editing process. Also used during sweetening. A film copy is sometimes referred to as a "slop print." Video copies with Burn-In Time Code are known as "window dubs."

Workstation: Refers to a disk-based audio recording/editing system. See Digital Audio Workstation.

Photo Credits

page vii, Ralph Nelson, courtesy of Columbia Pictures
page 3, courtesy of Looking Glass Films
page 4, courtesy of LucasArts Entertainment
page 5, THE GODFATHER Copyright ©1972 by Paramount Pictures. All Rights
Reserved.
page 9, "STAR WARS"™ & © Lucasfilm Ltd. (LFL) 1977. All Rights Reserved.
page 10, Peter Da Silva
page 11, Ralph Nelson, courtesy of Columbia Pictures
page 13, courtesy of James G. Stewart
page 15, courtesy of James G. Stewart
page 16, courtesy of the Lilly Library, Indiana University
page 19, © Orion Pictures Corp.
page 20, Greg Orloff photo courtesy of Skywalker Sound/LucasArts Entertainment
page 31, © Carolco/Tri-Star Pictures Inc.
page 32, © Carolco/Tri-Star Pictures Inc.
page 34, courtesy of Skywalker Sound/LucasArts Entertainment
page 37, © Warner Bros. Inc.
page 38, © Warner Bros. Inc.
page 41, © Warner Bros. Inc.
page 43, © The Walt Disney Company
page 45, © The Walt Disney Company
page 46, © The Walt Disney Company
page 49, THE HUNT FOR RED OCTOBER Copyright © 1990 by Paramount Pictures.
All Rights Reserved.
page 55, © New Line Cinema Corp.
page 56, © New Line Cinema Corp.
page 58, "LAST CRUSADE"™ & © Lucasfilm Ltd. (LFL) 1989. All Rights Reserved.
page 60, Halina Krukowski/LucasArts Entertainment
page 63, © 20th Century Fox Film Corp.
page 64, © 20th Century Fox Film Corp.
page 67, © Tri-Star Pictures Inc.
page 69, © Tri-Star Pictures Inc.
page 70, © Tri-Star Pictures Inc.
page 71, © Tri-Star Pictures Inc.
page 79, © Promotour U.S. Inc./BCL Productions
page 80, Elizabeth Annas
page 95, © 20th Century Fox Film Corp.
page 97, © 20th Century Fox Film Corp.
page 99, © CBS-TV Inc.
page 100, © CBS-TV Inc.
page 101, Richard Maddox
page 102, courtesy of Skywalker Sound/LucasArts Entertainment
page 104, © Capital Cities/ABC Inc.
page 106, © Capital Cities/ABC Inc.
page 109, © Capital Cities/ABC Inc.
page 110, © Capital Cities/ABC Inc.
page 112, © Paramount Pictures Corp.
page 115, © Paramount Pictures Corp.
page 117, Terry Stark
page 118, Ed Freeman
page 119, Terry Stark
page 122, Terry Stark
page 125, George Petersen

Acknowledgments

Special thanks to Richard Beggs, Antonia Coffman at Fox-TV, Don Drake, Steven J. Epstein, Dana Friedman and Kristin Fain at Arsenio Hall Communications Ltd., Karen Gilbert at Zoetrope, George Hernandez at Capital Cities/ABC Inc., Rebecca Herrera at Twentieth Century Fox Film Corp., Halina Krukowski at Lucasfilm, Michael Lynton at Disney Publishing Group, Larry McCallister at Paramount Pictures, Ann McColgan at LucasArts, Carolyn McMaster, Miles Perkins at Industrial Light and Magic, George Petersen, Chrissy Quesada at Carolco Pictures, Sonia Thompson at NewLine Cinema, Theresa Tucker at Walt Disney Co., Michael Turner at Orion Pictures, Walter and Beatrice Murch at Looking Glass Films, John Michael Weaver at Loyola Marymount University, and Edward Zimmerman at Columbia Pictures Television.

Also Available From MIX BOOKS And ELECTRONIC MUSICIAN BOOK

CONCERT SOUND

Concert Sound takes you behind the boards with top touring acts and shows how the pros are doing it today! Featuring exclusive coverage on top sound reinforcement companies and over a dozen major touring acts including U2 Zoo TV, Tom Petty, AC/DC, Gloria Estefan and Dire Straits, it's a case study in how contemporary sound reinforcement is executed. With additional coverage of theaters and clubs for acts like k.d. lang, Lou Reed and Tori Amos; festival productions such as Rock in Rio, and Lollapalooza; safe rigging; monitor mixing; and drum miking. 128 pages.
00183016 $17.95

MAKING MUSIC WITH YOUR COMPUTER

from *Electronic Musician* magazine
edited by David Trubitt

Whether you're a computer user coming to grips with electronic music technology or a musician searching for the right computer, this new title will show you how to get started. It looks at the many ways computers contribute to the music-making process, then demystifies the bridge between the components: MIDI. It shows you how to choose the right computer and equipment for your specific needs and features the most popular types of software, including programs for recording and printing your music. It also explains digital audio, hard-disk recording, and music in multimedia applications. With additional tips on how to get software support and an extensive glossary of terms, you'll be well supported to use your computer for music. 128 pages.
00330056 $17.95

HAL BLAINE AND THE WRECKING CREW

by Hal Blaine with David Goggin

Ever wonder what it would be like to be the most recorded musician in popular music? This biography spotlights Hal Blaine, drummer extraordinaire, and his life experiences. From the Sinatras to the Beach Boys, Blaine drumrolled through the 50s, 60s and 70s, driving over 40 songs to the number one slot. His work with Phil Spector and the Wrecking Crew sessions, his touring experiences and other hit-making pressure sessions are amusingly revealed in this rare glimpse of a golden age. Exclusive scrapbook photos round out this biography to provide an entertaining and educational book for musicians and fans alike. 192 pages.
00330037 $19.95

MUSIC PRODUCERS

Conversations With Today's Top Record Makers, by the Editors of Mix.

Twenty four producers including Don Dixon (R.E.M), Bruce Fairbairn (Aerosmith), Daniel Lanois (U2), Bill Laswell (P.I.L.), Jeff Lynn (Tom Petty), George Martin (Beatles), Hugh Padgham (Sting), Phil Ramone (Billy Joel), Rick Rubin (Red Hot Chili Peppers), Don Was (Bonnie Raitt) and 13 others discuss how they got started, how they mediate between labels and artists, what equipment they prefer, analog/digital format decisions, how they "build" a mix and much more. These insights, p personal stories about conducting sessions with today's biggest names, ma this a valuable insider's guide to making records. 128 pages
00183004 $17.95

ELECTRONIC MUSICIAN'S TECH TERMS

A Practical Dictionary for Audio and Music Production
by Petersen & Oppenheimer

Stay on top of technology with this new resource from the pr editors of *Mix* and *Electronic Musician* magazines. In additic all the standard definitions, this new dictionary covers the l terms you need to understand digital audio, workstations, com music and home recording technologies. 56 pages.
00330055 $9.95

SOUND FOR PICTURE:

An Insider's Look At Audio Production In Film And Television by the editors of Mix

Takes you behind the scenes as top sound professionals reveal how dialog, sound effects and musical scores are recorded, edited and assembled into seamless soundtracks. Exclusive case studies spotlight blockbusters like *Terminator 2, Malcolm X, The Simpsons, The Doors, Twin Peaks* and many others. Focuses on both the philosophical and technical sides of sound design. With foreword by Francis Ford Coppola and a full glossary, this new book is ideal for audio engineers, recording students, aspiring sound operators, and cur film and video buffs alike. 140 pages.
00330054 $17.95

Prices and availability subject to change without notice. Some books may not be available outside the U.S.A.

For more information, see your local music dealer, or write to:
Hal Leonard Publishing Corporation
P.O. Box 13819 Milwaukee, Wisconsin 53213